Reflections on Life
Pastor Ponderings

David P. Mays

LUCAS PARK BOOKS
ST. LOUIS, MISSOURI

Copyright © 2010 David P. Mays

All rights reserved. No part of this book may be reproduced or transmitted in any form or by any means, electronic or mechanical, including photocopying, recording, or by any information storage and retrieval system, without permission in writing from the copyright owner. For permission or to reuse content, please contact dmays@dkjjt.com.

All photographs and drawings are the sole property of David and Katherine Mays, 1970-.

Scripture quotations marked (RSV) are taken from the "Revised Standard Version of the Bible, copyright 1952 [2nd edition, 1971] by the Division of Christian Education of the National Council of the Churches of Christ in the United States of America. Used by permission. All rights reserved."

Scripture quotations marked (NRSV) are taken from the "New Revised Standard Version Bible, copyright 1989, Division of Christian Education of the National Council of the Churches of Christ in the United States of America. Used by permission. All rights reserved."

Scripture quotations marked (NIV) are taken from the Holy Bible, New International Version®, NIV®. Copyright © 1973, 1978, 1984 by Biblica, Inc.™ Used by permission of Zondervan. All rights reserved worldwide.

Scripture quotations marked (KJV) are taken from The King James Version Electronic Database. Copyright © 1988-2006, by Biblesoft, Inc. All rights reserved.

Library of Congress Control Number: 2010930680
ISBN: 978-1-60350-008-1

Published by Lucas Park Books
www.lucasparkbooks.com

Written with a pastor's heart and a counselor's sensibilities, David prepared this book during a time of personal transition and introspection. Call it cathartic, call it theological reflection, call it a devotional guide-- this book is a heartwarming collection of short stories reminding everyone of God's undying love.

I believe you will find a meaningful connection between *your* story and David's.

Dr. Mark Bushor, pastor
Central Christian Church
Killeen, Texas

Acknowledgements

 I developed the thoughts and method for this book while involved in Clinical Pastoral Education (CPE), in a class by Joe Gross, at Veterans Hospital in Dallas. I thank Joe and the other class members who struggled with me in finding God in everyday events. The class, based on a book by Abigal Johnson, *Reflecting on God*[1] provided a mechanism for the discovery. If this book is useful and you would like to learn more about discovering God in daily life, I recommend Johnson's book.

 I would not have completed this project without the continued support of friends and family. John, my son, put together some of the stories I had written in a picture book to incentivize me. He called it a book of his favorites and gave it to me as a Christmas present. It was a book of colors for me! Invaluable in the process as well was my sister Susan Green and cousin Bobby Mays who spent countless hours editing. To my friend Mark Bushor checked my theology. To Joel Craw who published a book of poems, *From the Heart*, written by his grandfather Howard Allen Craw, which my youngest son loved, this prodded me to record some of my stories.

 My thanks also, to friends Davin Chapman, Carl Jacobs, Bill Hurlbut and everyone in Pickton, Texas along with countless others for providing fodder for my stories. Thanks to my son, Joe, and wife, Kathy, for their photography, art and encouragement. I recognize that one person never accomplishes a project such as this. Our lives are intertwined and mingled such that joys and pain of one may be seen in another. All I did was write some of them down.

---

[1] Abigail Johnson, *Reflecting with God : Connecting Faith and Daily Life in Small Groups* (Herndon, Va.: Alban Institute, 2004).

Table of Contents

Reaching out to God   1
  Sharing a Meal with God   1
  What is in a Name?   2
  Setting the Context   3
  I Shall Not Want   5
  Finding what you Seek   6
  Marveling   7

The Christian Thing   10
  Getting the Car Fixed   10
  Driving in the Fast Lane   11
  Want a Ride?   12
  The Kingdom of God   13
  Hidden in Plain Sight   15
  A Song of Recollection   17
  What do you like about Worship?   18
  Character of Friends   19
  The Pains and Blessings of Waiting   20
  Moving   21
  How to Tell a Story   22

Keeping a "Right" Attitude   24
  Bobblehead Jesus   24
  Independence Day   26
  Using the "Right" tool   27
  Wow Moments   28
  Unpacking   30
  Peppermint Tea   31
  Saddle Racks   32

Old becomes new	33
Is it worth it?	34
Groundbreaking	35
The Rose of Attention	37
What can Music do?	39
What is on Your List?	40
How Much Information is Enough?	41
What's in a Smile?	42
I am ALWAYS right	43
What is really important	**46**
Casting Lots	46
Responding in the Face of Fear	47
Preoccupation	48
To God be the Glory	49
Peering into the Atom	50
Don't Touch that Handle	52
Flying off the Handle	53
Momma Mays' Rolls	55
Got Plans?	57
Building Community	58
Watermelons	60
Colorado	**62**
Half Moon Campground	62
Alpine Tunnel	63
Courage in the Face of Adversity	65
Experiencing Something New	67
Staying the Course	69
Finding Rest	71
Christmas Seasons	**73**
Is it Fall or Autumn?	73
Anniversary	75

Who took Baby Jesus?	76
Christmas Pud	77
The Book of Color	79
Lent	81
The Trailer	81
Getting the Lint out of Lent	82
Changing Times	85
Dexter	85
A New Way	87
Waiting in Line	88
Pecking for Freedom	90
Finding the Truth	91
Lawn Mowers and Taxes	93
A Perfect Mother	94
Graduation	95
The Wooden Chair	97
There's More To It	98
Betrayal	99
The Call	101
Prayer Life	102
On the Road	103
Acts of Agape	104
A Piece of Chicken	106
Epilogue	109
Bibliography	110
Index	111

Reaching out to God

Sharing a Meal with God

She slipped quietly into the kitchen and over to the counter. She had finally grown tall enough, and stretching on her tiptoes, she could reach the back of the counter top. That is where the Graham Crackers were kept. She quickly put several into the small brown bag she had. Next to the box of crackers there was an opened chocolate bar. She broke off several pieces and put them into the bag as well. She rolled the bag up and tightly pressed it against her so that nobody could see it and slithered out the back door of the house and into the yard.

With a house full of brothers and sisters, it was hard to get away from the noise, teasing and problems. Everyone was home that Saturday morning and she could feel the electricity in the air. Many things went wrong last night. She didn't want to be there when the tension clapped like thunder and voices rumbled through the house. Why does it have to be this way, she wondered.

Behind the kitchen, just down the steps, there was on open crawl door that went under the house. It was dark and creepy under the house, but she knew she could be alone. She didn't like the dark, so she found a place next to the opening and sat with her bag in her lap. If she just knew what to pray for, she would. She just wanted to find peace.

When our lives are in discord, it is hard to see a way to peace. We care for all those around us and we wonder how strife seems to come from all around, even from those we love and respect. Paul tells us "We do not know what we ought to pray for, but the Spirit himself intercedes for us with groans that words cannot express."(Romans 8:26 NIV)

She sat with tears in her tightly closed eyes, not thinking, not wanting, just waiting. She waited for God to be with her. After a moment, she wiped her tears on her sleeve, rolled open the bag, and took the crumpled crackers and chocolate. She gave thanks for God's presence and ate.

What is in a Name?

PPL @TEOTD TPTB w@ 2 knw, dz NE1 knw d nme of God.

WAM WWJD FYI cll God dad. O*-)[1]

We call God by many different names; Jehovah, Yahweh, Lord, Elohim, I am, Adonai, The Mighty One, The Father and Abba. The Jewish people call God by YHWH, G_d or The Lord because they are not allowed to speak the name of God. In Exodus 3 God calls Moses in the burning bush. God tells Moses he is on sacred ground and states clearly who He is. Moses was afraid to look at God. Later Moses starts to negotiate with God and requests God's name. God responded, "I am who I am," or as one Jewish professor explained it, God said, "I am not going to tell you my name."

When someone demands your name, that person seeks to have control or power over you. Moses was seeking a way to improve his position and power by pretending he did not know God's name. Often we try to make deals with God in an effort to be in control. God, if you will do this I will do that. Save me now Lord and I will serve you. We need to be

---

[1]Interpretation -- PEOPLE! At the end of the day, the powers to be would like to know if anyone knows the name of God. Wait a minute, what would Jesus do – For your information – call God Dad. A smiling angel wearing sunglasses.

careful when we make a deal with God. We might just get what we asked for. When the Israelites demanded a King in 1 Samuel 8:6, they were warned that it was not a good idea. But they didn't let up. God provided Saul and they were unhappy with the way things turned out.

Often we discover that when God does not give us what we want, we did not need what we asked for in the first place. God provides what we need at an appropriate time. It is hard to see when we are up to our neck in disasters and problems, but later it becomes clear. This is one reason to journal your faith-walk. That way you can look back and see God's action in your life. It does not matter by which name you call God. God knows our hearts and our minds and loves us just as we are. We do the right thing when we give our lives to trusting God. **GBU (((H)))**[2]

Setting the Context

One weekend Kathy and I traveled to Fairhope, Alabama. We needed to get away and we wanted to go to a restaurant we visited seventeen years earlier with our son. The restaurant was on the Eastern side of Mobile Bay, just above Ft. Morgan. The sun would set and generate spectacular sunsets on the water between Ft. Morgan and Ft. Gaines at the mouth of Mobile Bay and the Gulf of Mexico. There was a cold front due to pass through the area and we felt it would heighten the experience.

The sunset was beautiful, but Hurricane Ivan or Katrina removed the restaurant. Not a trace was left. That was OK because we only came for the view. We experienced many unexpected blessings on the trip. We were rerouted south off of I-20 just before we got to Vicksburg, and the traffic was backed up for miles. We decided to leave the traffic and take back roads south through Natchez, Mississippi. Driving slower off the interstate gave us time to take in the spectacular views found along the way.

Traveling through a forest of trees, we noticed to the west a small glen. In the glen, there was a meadow with

---
[2]God be with you and lots of hugs.

a white church to one side. It had a sign that read, "The Church in the Wildwood." It was just as the song described and reminded me of a small church building I passed on Highway 80 many years before. I started to remember.

I was on my way to flight school in Savannah, Georgia. It was the first time away from home and I was a little nervous. It was early in the morning and the dew was fresh on the trees and bushes. I crossed an old steel bridge and it reminded me of a bridge back home. They both had low lying fog over the bottom land. After a few miles I spotted a graveyard and decided to stop and eat a sausage roll with a cup of coffee. As I walked towards the graveyard a small chapel of red cedar came into view. It seemed to be a perfect place to stop and have a conversation with God.

Music filled my head and I sang, "I come to the garden alone, while the dew is still on the roses."[3] In the middle of the graveyard I spoke a prayer of fear over what was surely to come in a few months, Vietnam and combat. Would I have to kill, would I die, would I ever see my family again? As I sat – slowly a peace came over me that everything was

[3] C. Austin Miles, In the Garden, 1913
[4] St. Andrew's Episcopal Church -Prairieville, Alabama

as it should be. I gained confidence that God was with me and I was not alone.

Kathy and I set out to relive a moment at a particular spot. But our journey turned out to be so much more. Because of work done by others I was able to remember and share things from my past. It is the faithful few that provide opportunities for moments of revelation. They clean up after the storm, they build the churches, they tend to the graveyards, and they are the ones that do what needs to be done without fanfare glory or honor. It is their actions that set a context for God to be revealed in our world. Are you one of the faithful few!

I Shall Not Want

A cold chill blew through the trees and the rushing wind tingled my skin reminding me I was alive. I remember that day, lying on my reclining lawn chair next to the creek. It was a day that, one might say, had not gone very well. As I lay quietly listening to the water run over the rocks with a gentle gurgle and pop, I could hear it leaving its worries and problems behind. I wondered if I could leave mine behind as well. The sound of the water was calming and I felt at peace with nature, God and myself. Why was I so calm after all the events of the day?

Our home was along Clear Creek, next to Wedding Woods west of Fayetteville. It sat down in a valley at the top of an open meadow that stretched to the water's edge. A grouping of trees formed a perfect camping spot. I liked to go there to reflect on life and read my Bible. I was reading Psalm 23 and I realized how the passage applied to my life.

Every verse was a current event in my life. I concentrated on the first verse, "The LORD is my shepherd, I shall not want." I shall not want ... hum ... I was calm and at peace because I did not want. Spiritual and mental pain comes when we want what we do not have. I realized that I had come to a point in my life where I trusted God to provide what I needed. I arose each day with excitement to see what God was doing and to revel in its delight. I was at peace because I was satisfied with what God had provided. Yes, with the Lord as my shepherd each day was a day of new beginnings. Thank you Lord for the cold chill of the rushing wind reminding me, "I AM ALIVE!"

Finding what you Seek

"Now David, you find what you seek," my mother would say every time I would complain about others. Years later, I finally realized just what that meant. It really hit home when I was doing research in robotics trying to determine how much information was required to recognize something. It seems the human brain fills in a lot of information without really, "seeing it". The brain uses past experience to fill in what it doesn't know.

For example, if I caught my boys acting a particular way then my brain would look back at my experiences and fill in the missing pieces. If I thought they were up to something, they were. I didn't know I was filling in with assumption. Most of the time, we are totally unaware we have filled in the missing pieces or rearranged the information. An obvious example of how we do this is to read part of a paragraph that has floated around the internet.

"It deosn't mttaer in waht oredr the ltteers in a wrod are, the olny iprmoatnt tihng is taht the frist and lsat ltteer be at the rghit pclae." We fill in, change and rearrange information that we see, read and hear. Therefore, if we think someone is wrong, he or she is wrong. It doesn't matter what really happened. Our minds will rearrange the information to fit our expected outcome. That is what my mother meant when she said, "You find what you are looking for." My past informs my present, which influences my future. This says that when I have a disposition to a subject matter it will affect how I see that matter. It is a choice I make, look for good or look for bad. I will find what I seek.

Saul bent on stamping out this movement called "The Way" searched out followers of Jesus who blasphemed the law – at least that was the way he saw it – until God called his hand. How often do we desire bad for others before we confirm the facts, validate our thoughts, or start over and look for good? Sometimes I think we need scales over our eyes to correct our vision so we may see the truth. (Acts 9) May God remove our scales so that we may see through the eyes of Christ and know the truth. What blocks your vision, thoughts and feelings from accepting others?

Marveling

Sunday afternoon is a time Kathy and I love to marvel, a tradition handed down from my mother. Often we end up where Kathy likes to marvel the most – antique shops. "For what are you looking," I ask. "I'll know it when I see it," she responds. I digress. Marveling is not just about antique shops. Let me return to task. Marveling is about knowing when it is seen. "What," you ask, is to be found so that it can be known? That is a bit trickier. The way mom taught to marvel is that you start out with a sharp eye for creation. It is to find God within God's creation. It might be something new or something that suddenly sprang to life for the first time, something you notice or come to see differently for the first time.

---

[5] A Swan, the summer of 2003 next to the Swan Hotel along the river Ouse in Bedford England

I can marvel at God's creation, seeing the beauty of contrast across the valley. I can marvel at the changes in soil alongside the roadway, where shovels have dug out the hill. I can marvel at the hawk swooping across the field. I can marvel at the swiftness of the deer leaping over the fence to safety. I can marvel at the look in a person's eyes when given a cup of coffee, ice cream cone, a "Thank you" or a word of encouragement. Marveling is being aware of God and giving God the credit for creation.

The next step is to take something that will remind us of that moment. A rock, small leaf, a napkin from the store, a toothpick to remember a flavor, a picture or whatever is placed in a small box and kept until Sunday at dinner the following week. Each person, in turn, takes out the item that represents their memory and shares it with the others so that they may also experience the event. It is an opportunity to experience God anew. At its best, marveling is discovering God in others.

Moments of marveling are responding to the call of the Holy Spirit. It is when we become sensitive to the presence of the Holy Spirit that marveling kicks into high gear. We start to look at others and find ways to help them discover the self within them. We become more hospitable and receptive. Having other people around creates opportunity to discover and open ourselves up as examples to others. It is in opening ourselves to others that we must learn self-control.

Self-control is remembering it is not about re-living our discovery. Marveling is not going around, finding how many people we can force into listening to our story. It is about holding our story until a moment when another person is struggling and looking for guidance. It is about sharing the bare basics of our own story to allow the other to speak, reflect and share about their story.

Our presence when others make discoveries is an act of marveling. After all, marveling is not about re-living the old; it is about discovering the new. Self-control is to be ready to do, say, act, remain silent, pray or whatever is required so that someone else may marvel at God's presence in their life. Self-control is where hospitality begins. It is creating a context of awareness and yearning, allowing others to marvel at God's creation and find themselves a part of that creation.

Marveling is about making Disciples by discovering God anew in our world. Consider how your experience, awareness, and hospitality can help those in your church and your community discover God in their lives. Take a moment and put a reminder in a box (your heart) and at the called moment take it out and share how God was found. Marvel at how God can use you to change our world. Marvel at God's new creation.

The Christian Thing

Getting the Car Fixed

One week I went to the Chrysler dealership to get my wife's Jeep serviced. I entered the service manager's area and noticed that he was helping a young lady with a small child. She was giving him her keys, then she left for the waiting area and he entered his office. After a few minutes, he motioned me to come into his office. I noticed the service manager's name was Chris.

We were discussing the work needed on my Jeep when his phone rang. There was a pause and Chris said, "I was hoping we could do this for free. She is a single mother and someone stole her keys. She is afraid someone will steal her car. She has already paid to have her other locks changed. Can't we do something?" There was a pause, "That much, huh." Another pause, "How much if I pay for it?" Pause. "OK, I'll pay for it."

The woman's car fixed with new locks she went on her way. She had no idea that Chris paid for it out of his own pocket. As far as she knew, Chrysler or the dealership paid for it. Chris saw a need, and without fanfare or credit helped someone. When I asked him why he paid for it he said, "It's the right thing to do."

Jesus taught about giving. It was part of the Sermon on the Mount just before the Lord's Prayer. "So when you give to the needy, do not announce it with trumpets ... do not let your left hand know what your right hand is doing." (Matthew 6:2-3 NIV) Chris was responding just as Christ taught. I thanked Chris for what he did and asked permission to write about this experience. He gave permission after hesitating. To everyone like "Chris", thanks for giving.

As part of the Church, we often do not beat our drums or play our trumpets when we act in the name of Christ. It makes for poor advertising but for good Christianity. In fact, many church members do things of which we are not aware. This changes how people find out about church and how they become members. Have you ever noticed something that "just got done?"

The best advertising is when we invite a neighbor or a friend to be a part of what we are doing. They get to know us and want to be a part of what we are doing. Many more trips are in the future, back to Chris for service because he had a good heart. I hope people have seen my heart and will want to become part of the church.

Driving in the Fast Lane

Two experiences stand in contrast – yet are the same. I was traveling on a four lane road south of town, bumping over railroad tracks and peering at mailboxes and buildings set back from the road trying desperately to read an address. Where is that place, I wondered. There are too many things on my plate today. I don't need this delay. With my mind, other places and my attention on finding a building I didn't notice the horde of cars coming up behind me. As they started swooping by, I heard a gentle toot–toot reminding me I was holding up traffic. I moved over and got out of everyone's way and the traffic moved again. That toot–toot made me aware that what I was doing was affecting others around me negatively. It made me glad there was not a Christian Church bumper sticker on my car.

The other experience was overhearing numerous church members excited about their church and telling others. They shared, expressed love, and showed concern for others. They accepted everyone even of vastly different life styles.

The Body of Christ was at work. I wish I had a bumper sticker on my forehead that said, CHRISTIAN CHURCH. I was proud to be a part.

When we slipup in life, God provides us a gentle toot–toot to make us aware. We need to look around and see what affect we are having on others. Then we can correct our actions. When we slipup in life we can also look around to see who else is present because God provides the Body of Christ to surround us with love reminding us that we are children of God. Look around at others and pay attention, toot-toot.

Want a Ride?

Watching and following my dad, as a young child, was how I learned life concepts. He was a sales supervisor for a milk company. The best part of working with dad was all the places we would eat. Most mornings started about five AM with breakfast at home, but sometimes we would drive to the dairy and eat at J.D. Crows. It was a restaurant next door to the dairy and most of the dairy workers would eat breakfast together. There was always lively conversation.

Each day's lunch would be a different experience. Like making my own Dagwood sandwich by going down the back of the meat counter in a grocery store, or a meat and three style diner in the middle of nowhere where strangers might share a table, or stopping in the country where someone had a pit in the ground with the most tender and flavorful barbeque. It seemed Dad knew everyone all over the state and all the best places to eat. Every place had its own clientele with different conversations to go with different foods.

Speaking of different foods, my grandmother was British, and when she came over to visit, we made trips to Simon-David where chocolate covered ants, roasted grasshoppers and such things were the item of the day. Mom would make toad-in-the-hole or yorkshire pud and roast beef. We had lamb when it could be found cheaply. And of course, there is nothing like Christmas pud.

You might say I didn't know what a restricted diet was. Raising my family, I wanted them to experience all the types of food possible just like their dad and importantly the people and conversations that went with the food. We might have Mexican, French, Indian, American Indian, Russian, Italian, Soul Food, Tex-Mex, Japanese, Chinese, Dim Sum or Australian cuisine to name a few. If we saw a restaurant of which we had never partaken, we would stop and try it. We discovered richness for our palate and for people. However, to do that, we had to experience some real bombs. Blessed by all the treats, even when we could not get it down, we were always thankful. A great variety of food gave a new passion to living, an excitement with expectation.

Michael Yaconelli writes, "Jesus came to forgive us of our sin, yes, but His mission was also to introduce us to the passion of living. Most people believe that following Jesus is all about living *right*. Not True. Following Jesus is all about living *fully*." Yaconelli writes it is a roller coaster ride of passion when "all you can do is hang on for life."[1] One of the rides is experiencing foods and others. More often than not, something will come up that allows me to share my faith or support someone else in his or her faith.

Kathy and I ate at the @1844, Inc. Café. We talked with the cook, owner and waitress. She said, "If you're going to eat here – you're going to hear about family." Sitting down to table and sharing lives, hopes and dreams can be a roller coaster ride of thought, interest and challenge. It creates a moment of living fully. I can imagine Jesus and others reclining at table sharing stories about life and living fully. Have you shared a meal with someone new? Have you had a chance to share your faith? Care for a ride? Imagine traveling in a milk truck, go find somewhere new and out of the way to experience life.

The Kingdom of God

It was about ten thirty and I was getting hungry. I stepped in a café that was open for breakfast, brunch and lunch and ordered fruit crepes with coffee. The coffee arrived and at

---

[1] Mike Yaconelli, *Dangerous Wonder : The Adventure of Childlike Faith*, [Rev. ed. (Colorado Springs, Colo.: NavPress, 2003).

the same time a woman, with three children sat in the booth next to me. Let us call them: Mom, Angela age nine, Marcie age six and the youngest Maria age five.

They all poured over the menus and Mom ordered for the group. Mom and Angela had their backs to me and I could not see their faces. The light was dim through the enormous wooden blind covered windows due to clouds in the sky. All sat quietly for the moment. I turned back to my crepes.

Mom said, "Oh look it's raining." Maria was the only one to look up. Angela appeared to be reading. Marcie was coloring the menu. She was sitting on her knees with her back to the group and the menu on the ledge of the window. She was deeply involved with the picture. Maria starred out the window. The pupils of her eyes were so large you could not tell what color her eyes were. She was motionless and fixated as if she were hypnotized. What was it that had her captivated?

Marcie turned to the group and pushed aside all that was in front of her to make room to place her picture on the table. She reached over, took the box of colors from in front of Maria and started to outline something. Maria did not respond at all, as she continued her stare. Gentle rain continued to soak street, cars, buildings and people that walked by the window.

Water and orange juice arrived. Maria looked up at the waitress, Marcie moved her painting back to the window ledge to make room for the drinks, and Angela reached out and took hers from the hands of the waitress and said, "Thank you." As Marcie turned to the ledge, she stopped, looked at the group and said, "O Look, it's raining." They all quietly turned and looked out the window.

Food was set on the table and all turned to their plates - bagels with jelly, syrup, cream cheese and fruit dishes. Maria didn't like what was on her plate, so mom exchanged items with her from her own plate. Marcie held her bagel in the air and licked the jelly off. Maria noticed she had two water glasses and announced the mistake to the whole group. "I can't have two glasses, Mom" she said. Mom moved one of the glasses and Maria was happy. She finished her meal and stated she was ready to go, then sat and pouted while the others continued to eat. The ticket arrived; Mom got up, left the group, and went to the cashier to pay. Maria found the fruit and was content with a full mouth.

Mom returned. Angela looked up at mom with loving eyes as she slid out the booth. Marcie gave Mom the picture she had colored and they all walked out the door into another world. They did not seem to be aware of how Mom paid or what the true cost of the meal was or where the funds came from, only that Mom paid. For them, the meal was free, life was good and Mom provided what they needed. Mom represents Christ, the children church members, inside the café is earth, those at other tables are part of the Body of Christ, and outside the door is Heaven.

When Christ was present, many did not hear what he said. Some came to serve, but were not part of the Body of Christ. Some were content in life to sit and watch, but not willing to commit. Some were a part, but focused mostly on themselves. Some wanted it all to be over when they were finished, but then found additional blessings in life. Some were a part, yet made secular things the greatest part of their lives. Some were content to "just be" in the presence of the master.

God provides nourishment, wonder, and relationship. God paid our bill through the gift of Jesus the Christ. God has invited all to come to the table. John tells us, "The Spirit and the Bride say, 'Come.' And let everyone who hears say, 'Come.' And let everyone who is thirsty come. Let anyone who wishes take the water of life as a gift." (Revelation 22:17 NRSV) God gave the blessing of Jesus and Jesus has paid our bill. We are free to get up and walk out the door to enjoy God's creation.

Hidden in Plain Sight

Whenever I have lost something and can't find it I say, "Well, I certainly put that in a safe place." Then I restart my

16 Reflections on Life

search, thinking it must be in plain sight because I did not find it in all my "hiding places". Things hidden in plain sight can be very difficult to find.

A very important item was part of a greater project. This small item was the key to unlocking a great difficulty. If only we could make it work. We studied, tested, connected, twisted, turned upside down and put it in backwards and it still gave errors. Hours upon hours spent trying to make this thing work. I thought, if I had it at home maybe I could reveal its secrets. After showing it around, I placed it in a "safe place" so the kids could not get to it.

The next morning, the "safe place" could not be located to retrieve this important part. I had to go to work without it. Every person that came by my desk brought fear and anguish of being found out. All day long was filled with thoughts of what to say, how to cover up. Then the next and the next day turned to a week and then a month. Deadlines were looming and still the part remained lost. I turned the house upside down. Nights became sleepless torture of looking and not finding.

Finally, in desperation, I prayed acknowledging my lies, misdirection and cover-up. God heard the prayers of a lost man and collapse and rest came easy. After a few hours, in the still of the night, I awoke and looked up at the bookshelf I had gone through at least a hundred times. There in plain sight sat the part. It was in a greenish grey box blended in next to a greenish grey Bible.

It was one of those things so obvious that it hides in plain sight. Sometimes we think we know something so well that we miss it entirely. There are several good interpretations for the passages in Matthew 13 where Jesus talks about the Kingdom of Heaven. "The kingdom of heaven is like treasure hidden in a field, which someone found and hid; then in his joy he goes and sells all that he has and buys that field." (Matthew 13:44NRSV) One way to interpret this passage is look back at verse 38. The earth is the field and we are the good seed sown therefore we are the treasure found. Many have read these passages. Few have considered us as the treasure. God loves us so much that God gave everything to have a relationship with us. We are God's treasure. Are you spending your time looking at the books and missing what is in plain sight? Open your heart and let your spirit feed your thoughts – see God and know God loves you.

A Song of Recollection

Hoping for a quick sale on our home, I did a lot of repairs and maintenance. As I reflect back over the last months of seven day work weeks to get everything done, I realize why I felt tired, worn out, and alone. Often we let the constraints of the world push us into not taking any time for ourselves and sometimes we leave out God. This type of activity isolates us in the middle of a crowd. When we have enough, we call out to God in anguish. Like the Psalmist, "O God, thou art my God, I seek thee, my soul thirsts for thee; my flesh faints for thee, as in a dry and weary land where no water is." (Psalm 63:1 RSV) Where are you, why aren't you helping!

When we find ourselves at the bottom and all drained out, it may be that a phrase, or a piece of a song is all we can muster. When I feel like this, I remember songs like: *Lord Prepare Me To Be A Sanctuary, Like A Dear Panteth For The Water, All Hail The Power Of Jesus Name, I Will Lift Up My Hands In Your Name, Seek Ye First The Kingdom Of God, On The Wings Of A Snow White Dove, Praise Him Praise Him, All Through The Night,* and *If Ever I Loved You Lord Jesus T'is*

Now. We learn songs to help us know about God. We learn songs to help soothe our souls. What song comes to mind when you read/hear Psalm 63? What songs come to mind when you are tired, weary and alone?

Songs may remind us of events or times in our lives. When I hear the words "If ever I loved you – Lord Jesus t'is now," I hear them in harmony with a soprano and an alto, my sister and her friend Kay singing together. It brings joy to my heart and rekindles my fire. Now that most of the work has been finished and our house is listed on the market, I have the joyous feeling of "Praise God from whom all blessings flow."

How do you feel today? What song is on your heart? What song gives you joy? We must seek these feelings out and set aside time to reflect and remember. Take some time for yourself this week. Take some time for God this week.

What do you like about Worship?

One Sunday I asked a group as they were leaving church what they liked about the worship service. Answers were varied and surprising. One said, "I really liked the music. It was upbeat." The next one said, "Oh, I didn't like the music." I asked, "What was it about the music you didn't like," "We didn't sing, *Up From the Grave He Arose.*" The next said, "I liked putting the flowers on the cross" and another said, "I liked the sermon." One stated, "I liked it when you had to apologize and ask forgiveness from the sound engineer for walking in the wrong spot." The list went on and was as varied as the number of people.

We all come to worship/church for different reasons. The Psalmist says, "May God be gracious to us and bless us and make his face shine upon us, that your ways may be known on earth, your salvation among all nations." (Psalm 67:1-2 NIV) I come to worship each week to acknowledge God's presence in my life. I try to make known God's ways so that people are aware of God's salvation offered to all.

One Easter Sunday there was a great front that passed through my life clearing the fog of the world blocking my vision of God and God's ways for my life. I pray that each of you may also experience the clearing breath of the Holy Spirit in your life as you reflect on the gift of worship.

Character of Friends

I have a friend that came and visited one week. He drove a long way just to have lunch and then go back home. One Saturday, I drove a long way to have lunch, meet new friends and learn something about the church. Sometimes we need to go out of our way just to say, "Hi." At both of these events both parties had to go out of their way for each other even though only one traveled. People travel to come to church and we open our arms in loving support going out of our way.

In the letter to the Philippians it says, "Do nothing out of selfish ambition or vain conceit, but in humility consider others better than yourselves." (Philemon 2:3 NIV) I think Paul is asking us to give others the benefit of the doubt and to be open-minded. Paul asks us to go out of our way. It implies that we must use care when stating our position on a topic.

It seems to be so much easier to just let others "Know where we stand" than to listen and dialogue. When we "state the facts" instead of listening, we are showing our selfish ambition. Friends let us get away with it because they know us. Others see it as a challenge, as belittlement or disrespectful. When we fail to dialogue and state the facts, it is really done out of fear. We implement the thought that the best defense as a great offense. We make an offensive blitz and try to close the conversation. Doing this is the opposite of what Paul asks of us.

We have to struggle with our pride and value to consider others better than ourselves. My best friend, my wife Kathy, helps me to be aware when I am not humble. It is what good friends do. Good friends give of themselves freely and can be trusted to be honest and loving. If you love someone, you let them know when their ambition and conceit gives an air of superiority. We are all guilty at one time or another, so don't take it too badly.

"What does the LORD require of you but to do justice,

and to love kindness, and to walk humbly with your God?" (Micah 6:8 NRSV) Go out of your way for someone today and spend some time listening.

The Pains and Blessings of Waiting

What do you do when you are waiting? We all have times we must wait: in the doctor's office, at red lights, our turn in the bathroom. We wait for dinner, we wait for church to start and we wait for the flowers to grow. When I wait, I watch other people wait. Some read a book, others have video games, and some talk on cell phones and some talk to – well, I don't really know who they are talking to. Some sit, and from the look on their face, they are worrying about something or everything. Some just try to keep the little ones from getting into trouble.

In the book, *The Cup of Our Life* by Joyce Rupp, there is a chapter on the Mended Cup. Rupp starts the chapter with a quote from Christin Weber. "Waiting is endless ... I wait because I am powerless to do anything else. I wait because what I most treasure is what is deepest within and protected by silence. Out of waiting comes patience. Out of accepting my powerlessness comes strength and love and the courage to dare."[2]

It is like waiting for a wound to heal. At first, we are very aware of our wound with little to do to make it heal. We have to wait. Like the time I smashed my finger with a hammer. At first, every time I used my finger I remembered the blow it took. After a while, I started to use the finger and not even notice it was hurt. Soon I forgot the hammer blow completely. A time passed, I removed my fingernail, and now I wait for the nail to grow. I have gotten use to what my finger looks like and will wake up one day to a new fingernail. I will not really know when it arrived. Yet all the while I wait, something is happening.

We learn that we have to wait. We are powerless to change or speed up some things. If we are patient in our

---

[2]Joyce Rupp and Jane Pitz, *The Cup of Our Life : A Guide for Spiritual Growth* (Notre Dame, Ind.: Ave Maria Press, 1997).

waiting we can find times and places where we may have the courage to dare. We can dare to share our hopes. We can dare to share our faith with someone who is searching. We can dare to invite others to be a part of the waiting and anticipation. We can dare to grow the Body of Christ while we wait for the return of Christ. One day, we will awake to a new world. We are powerless to set the date. We should use this time to find the courage to dare.

Moving

Moving is a great thing for someone else to do. I can say that now that I am finished moving for the twentieth time, not counting in and out of storage. We started by packing all we could in one twenty six foot truck and moved it to storage. Next, a second twenty six foot truck was loaded. It seems as though there is no end to the things to be packed. Looking at each box wondering, "Is this really necessary?" We signed the papers selling our home, after everything was moved. Now we are homeless, interesting word, "homeless." Most of us are three paychecks from homeless. If someone looses their job through layoff, sickness, divorce or relocation, they may be homeless in just a few weeks. Now a days it is hard to find a job if you do not have an address and phone number. When people find themselves in that spot, homeless they become and homeless they stay.

I sat in my office, one last time, looking out over the field. Cattle and horses were grazing and a soft breeze rustled through the trees and bushes. I am going to miss this place, which seems strange remembering how much I did not want to move here. Nearly ten deals went south before we could do anything. It seemed as though this was the last place in town. Now, I realize how much God blessed us with this home even though it was an anxious wait.

The Israelites arrived in the desert and probably missed their homes. After so many years in slavery, many must have grown accustomed to their homes and the country. It could not have been all bad. Abraham went to Egypt to weather out the famine and then later Jacob went down to Egypt during a famine, each time finding an easy life. Jacob finding Joseph stayed and after Joseph died the enslavement started. Now, with Moses, the Israelites were back in the desert. Their caravans were full of wealth from the Exodus. Having all that stuff, they forgot God delivered them from slavery. In a moment of revelry, they pooled their gold to worship an image they created. (Exodus 31:1)

Kathy and I look forward to our own promised land. We have learned from the Israelites, and remember God provided. It was not the work of our own hands. Otherwise, we may find ourselves wandering for forty years in a nomadic homeless state like the Israelites. It is easy to forget the source of our strength and wealth. It is easy to take an attitude of "I got mine, let them get theirs," drawing a line between them and us. When we draw that line, we have worshipped the golden calf. I pray that God will help us to remember God's mighty works in our lives.

How to Tell a Story

James asked me the other day if I knew the difference between the way a northern story started and a southern story started. I confessed I did not know. He said, "A northern story always starts, 'Once upon a time' and a southern story starts, 'You aint gonna believe this.'" I smiled and acknowledged that he was correct to the best of my memory.

We learn ways to listen to what people say by how they start a conversation. Sometimes we try to understand what they mean. We recognize the fact that communication is often much more than words. We look at facial expressions, listen to the tone of voice and any other clues we might glean to understand shared information.

When someone starts out and says, "Once upon a time" we recognize a fictitious story with that single piece of information. The story might be based on real facts and may have meaning in our lives, even if only for entertainment. We gear up to hear differently based on what we hear first. Jesus might say, suppose one of you had a friend or a man was going down from Jerusalem to Jericho and we gear up to learn something important that is applicable to our lives. Yet we recognize that it is most likely a created event.

Personally, I like to start important stories in the pattern of Jesus. I like using "suppose" or "What would you say, if ..." sometimes I start with, "if this story ain't true it oughta be." This should gear the listener up to listen with an attentive ear of interpretation rather than an entertaining ear.

Suppose a young man went hunting with his uncle and his uncle's old bird dog named Bill. They walked for a long time. Every now and then Bill would stop and point and the uncle would shoot in the air. After several times like this the young man said, "What's going on." The uncle said, "You don't think I'm going to call Bill a liar after all we've been through do you."[3]

Reflecting on my life, I realize that often I remember things wrong, get them backward, or just mix multiple stories together. I am glad that my friends and family smile and nod their head. God has loved us and walked with us our whole lives. We have recognized God's love and in turn have loved God. Our lives are full of experiences. Sometimes we get life wrong and we make mistakes without even realizing that we were wrong. Like the uncle shooting his gun to signal approval of Bill, I think God is still proud of us and signals approval to shore us up.

Paul says in Galatians, "The only thing that counts is faith expressing itself through love." (Galations 5:6 NIV) I think that God has faith in us and loves us. That knowledge allows us to move forward. We try to live our lives in faith and in love with God and – to God – it counts. In Ephesians, we find, "In him and through faith in him we may approach God with freedom and confidence." Know today that God loves you and can see past your faults. Look for God's signal of approval in your life.

---

[3] A story I remember from my childhood, it is not a true story.

Keeping a "Right" Attitude

Bobblehead Jesus

They say the apple doesn't fall far from the tree. It is an interesting thought. We say it and laugh. We say, "I'm not anything like my father," "I'm not anything like my mother"

or "I'm not anything like my brother or sister." We say it in fun and in fear. We look at other family members, we know them so well because they are just like us, we see all their faults and we certainly do not want to be like them. That is the greatest problem with loved ones and us. It is easier for us to see each other's faults than strengths than our own. It is part of our human nature to seek out fault before strength. Finding a fault makes us look better. Practically speaking it is always easier to tear down a building than it is to build one.

Preparing a site for a new building, a bulldozer removed an old building in a matter of minutes. It was gone and buried. No trace left. I wonder how many hours were spent building that home so quickly destroyed. Relationships are the same way. We can tear down a relationship in a heartbeat, it takes time to rebuild, renew or restore. It is sad that when trouble happens we tend to find fault rather than strength. We tend to tear down rather than repair.

Sitting on my desk, next to my monitor, is a "Bobblehead Jesus" given to me by my son. He gave it to me with the instructions, "Remember to lighten up." Yes, the apple doesn't fall far from the tree, he is just like me. O Lord, I pray for him now. But! Wait. If he is like me, then I am like my dad, and he is like my granddad and him like my great granddad, and so on and so on. In effect when I look at my son I am looking at my great granddad and I am getting to know someone I have never met, seen or been around. I am getting to know who I am by looking at my children.

When my children were growing up and something would happen I would always (well some of the time) think back and say, "If I was their age and in this spot what would help me?" By understanding myself a little bit more it helped me raise my children. I can see my wife and her family member's resemblances in my children as well. I have discovered this to be a good thing. We can look at our past, to identify the bad traits and try to break the cycle of faults. As well, we can stroke and support those qualities we admire. However, to do that, we have to know ourselves and be brazenly honest and straightforward about what we find.

In Exodus 34 it says, God will have steadfast love for the thousandth generation and problems only to the third and the fourth generation. Thus anything good over the last four thousand years that happened in my family tree blesses me and all my bad stuff disappears by the time of my great-grand children. In the long haul, that is not bad progress. There is a two hundred fifty to one chance things will get better. That gives a lot of room for hope. We can all hear the message from my son, "Lighten up" and my wife adds, "And you will get a more harmonious outcome", a line we learned from the movie *Crossfire Trail*.

Jesus taught the Pharisees to "lighten up". They had twisted their understanding of the law and God's love so much that no one was happy. Everything was about tearing down, not building up; it was about isolation not inclusion. It was all about rules not relationships. I think Jesus would like my "Bobblehead Jesus." Therefore, I will "Lighten up" and love and build up the person God created.

Independence Day

What comes to mind when you think about Independence Day? For most of us it's shooting off fireworks or watching a cork float in the water. Hot dogs and baseball are also high on the importance list. Some watch traffic as they travel to and from loved ones homes, the beach or camping. For many, July 4th is just a day off.

Thinking back to the origin of the 4th, people had come from many places to gather in this new land. Some were escaping religious persecution, some were seeking fortunes and others wanted a new start, just an opportunity for a "Do Over" with their lives. Many reasons, many desires and many different visions and ways of life all together in one place. There were problems, disagreements and persecutions. The very thing that most wanted to change was starting all over again in their new land.

Then it happened! Fifty-five people came together and put their names, property, families and lives on the line to say, "Enough is enough." Fifty-five people listed our grievances and drew a line in the sand. Fifty-five people were willing to stand up for what they felt was the right thing to do. It was no longer acceptable to them to just follow and get along. Because fifty-five signed their name on our Declaration of Independence, not only did they change their lives, but the lives of a whole country. Not only a whole country but a whole world has changed as a result of their actions.

Another time in another place, a few came together and it changed the world. It began with twelve willing to sign up with Jesus. From those humble beginnings, Christianity blossomed. Another time it was only one. Ananias did not want to go and see Saul. Ananias knew about Saul and the evil Saul was doing to Christians. Ananias had a vision and responded to his call. He went as one and laid hands on Saul. (Acts 9:17) One person responded to God's call and acted in the face of adversity and the church was forever changed.

How do we change the world? We start by changing ourselves, by accepting ourselves as God's creation and trusting God for guidance, wisdom and courage. After we have made a change in our own lives, a change will happen in our family. When change has happened in our family, a change will take place in our neighborhood and then our city, state, country and the world. It sounds simple, but it all starts with one person standing up for the right thing. Look around. What is not fitting? What injustice can you see? Are you willing to step up and take action for independence and freedom?

Using the "Right" Tool.

Each hurricane season there is always something in short supply. Many projects go on hold for the lack of a very small part. In today's global economy, the problem increases because the small part may be in another country. During one part of my life, I built computer equipment and half our work was for foreign countries and companies. Getting parts and supplies across borders was always a difficult task. Some projects were very delicate operations that produced huge results. For example, an oil well in Canada went from ten barrels a day to two hundred barrels a day. Therefore, delays were costly.

One project was north of Dewberry, Alberta in Canada. We had shipped all of our equipment up and the installers called and said they found a leak. We sent new seals to stop the leak. The seals were very small rings of rubber about the size of a fingernail. It took over a week to ship. Then another leak and another set of rings. This went on set after set. Finally, I put ten seals in my pocket, got on an airplane and personally took them to the field.

I handed the installer a new set of rings and he pulled out a twenty-four inch pipe wrench to tighten the fitting. That is like someone coming in a big eighteen-wheeler truck to carry your grocery sack home. When the man put that huge wrench on my tiny fitting I said, "If you don't mind, I would like you to use this. As I handed him a small wrench, and just finger tighten, problem solved. In the oil patch, workers were used to working with big pipe that required big tools. The large wrench was what was handy it was what was easy.

When the Spirit moves us to share what God has done in our lives, sometimes we dump our WHOLE story when all that was needed is a short sentence. In Galatians, Paul speaks of a "spirit of gentleness." (Galations 6:1 NRSV) I believe that is how we are to treat one another, gently, lovingly with a kind and welcoming heart. Sometimes with very busy schedules and pressure from work, gentleness is in short supply.

When we visit people in their home, we sometimes feel like we need to take a whole sermon or a complete update of everything that has happened over the last year. When all we need is a short sentence. Taking communion to people at home is a gentle token that reconnects people to the church. Communion is a short sentence. It is just enough.

If you feel disconnected from the church, we miss you and hope to see you in church again. Come and receive just a word. Come and share communion. Little things can make a big difference.

Wow Moments

Most of us, as children, can remember at one time or another getting caught taking a cookie or a piece of candy when no one was looking. I remember playing in the backyard and smelling chocolate chip cookies in the oven. We didn't have air-conditioning, and the windows and doors were always open. We had screen doors to keep the flies out, and I liked to run in and out, banging the doors, getting in trouble every time.

Whenever I smelled cookies, I would wait several minutes and sneak around the side of the house to look in the window and see if they were on the counter and if mom had left the room. If she had – I would ever so carefully open the screen door, and quietly as a mouse, slip across the floor to the kitchen. I would wait and listen to make sure she was busy in the back of the house. Then, I would reach for a cookie. It never failed – as soon as I reached mom would call out, "Don't eat those cookies. They are for dinner." How did she do that? It wasn't just eyes in the back of her head; she had them posted in other rooms. I felt like she was watching me and could see my hand reaching for the cookie jar.

My parents knew what I was going to do before I thought about it. Later, as a parent, I discovered part of the secret. I just thought about what I would do as a child, and sure enough, my boys were out doing that very thing. Yet, it was also more than that. By watching them, I learned their patterns, what they liked and what they didn't like. It helped me to predict what was going to happen, or figure out what had just happened. I was never as good as my mother. She had a gift.

Today, I take a completely new approach to that same thought. Instead of watching for what my boys do wrong, I watch for the good things they do in their lives. It feels a lot better this way. I hear what they say when they are upset. I don't have to say anything because I know they will end up doing the right thing. Being aware of them working out their problems gives me a wow moment.

I wonder if God feels that way about us. The psalmist says, "Before a word is on my tongue you know it completely." (Psalm 139:4 NIV) The psalmist asks God to search and know their heart and to lead them in the way everlasting. Each day, I ask God to do this for me and I pray that what I do will give God a wow moment. I pray that God will ingrain on my heart the right thing so that I can do it without thinking. I think we all want to give God wow moments. This should be our prayer, "Lord, help me to give you a 'wow' moment." The Psalmist also tells us there is nowhere we can go without God. That gives us confidence and courage in what we do and say. It changes our whole attitude when we remember that God is always with us. Do you know that God is with you? Are you giving God wow moments? After all, created in the image of God, you are a chip off the ol' block.

Unpacking

I carefully lifted the box up on the table. I took my pocketknife and moved along the top edges and then down the center, lifting the flaps up and away to reveal the contents. It was the last box to open in my office. I peered inside to see what treasures I have not seen in the last eight months. There were scales, like the scales of justice, to remind me to balance my thoughts and to weigh them carefully.

Also inside, a few of mom's Bibles. I thumbed through and read some of her uncanny reflections and assignments of scripture to individuals. The one she assigned to me was Psalm 91. I remembered that she prayed this passage each day for me while I was in Vietnam.

Next was the car my son put together his last weeks in the hospital. It was broken. How could I have packed it so carelessly as to let it get broken? It was the last thing that my son made before his death. Maybe one of my sons can repair it. I hope so.

Moving seems to always bring reflections, sorrow and joy. It is a mixed bag of goods. I realize that I must often move and clean my memories and attitudes in life. It makes me wonder about the Disciples. What were their thoughts as they prepared their documents we now call The Gospels?

Pains and joys of life often come in reflections; our hope comes in what is ahead. We have a glimpse of hope as we open the flaps back and peer inside. We see what has been handed down through the generations for us in scripture and reflections on scripture. It is a sure hope packed carefully. "I will say of the Lord, 'He is my refuge and my fortress, my God, in whom I trust.' Surely he will save you from the fowler's snare and from the deadly pestilence. He will cover you with his feathers, and under his wings you will find refuge; his faithfulness will be your shield and rampart. (Psalm 91:2-4 NIV). That gives me comfort and courage. What do you feel when you open the Bible and read?

Peppermint Tea

Peppermint tea -- that is what my sister served the time Dad got angry. But it didn't make any sense. Why was he angry over peppermint tea? My sister had been preparing meals for about three months when Dad said, "That's it I've had all I can take." It just didn't make any sense. Dad seemed to be so upset. The rest of the meal was great. Dad talked about my sister on more than one occasion that summer to other people, about how proud he was of her, how she was doing such a good job while mom was gone. All the time he praised her, I didn't understand why was he upset this time over peppermint tea.

Many times, I wondered about that day, and many times, I teased my sister about peppermint tea. Later in life, I reflected deeply on the events of that day. Kathy, my wife, was in England for a few weeks with mom, and I at home with the three boys. Thinking about my situation, I discovered that Dad was not upset with my sister. It did not have anything to do with peppermint tea. You see, that summer mom had gone back to England to be with her mother because Granny Jessie was dying. Mom had been gone a long time. Dad was under stress of working long hours and taking care of three children when his wife was thousands of miles away. Dad was not angry, he missed mom.

When people act angry, it is rarely what we see that is the problem, and often we try to appease things by dealing with the obvious instead of taking the time to look around and discover the real problem. Peppermint tea became sweet tea, but Dad still missed mom. Dad was still proud of his daughter. I wish I had realized then. I wish I had not teased my sister so much. I pray she forgives me.

Jesus seemed to be so upset with Peter and said, "Get Behind me, Satan!" (Matthew. 16:23 NRSV) He said this just after telling Peter how proud he was of him. How do you think Peter felt? What was upsetting Jesus? Could these words have been about temptation? Jesus was still proud of Peter. Just a few days later, he took Peter to the transfiguration. Can you imagine that! Help us Lord not to react to things on the surface, but to wait for revelation so that we might understand and make a difference in your creation.

Saddle Racks

It was just six pieces of wood. Six pieces carefully crafted, shaped and formed. What was it I thought as I held it and imagined all the possibilities that I could fit on its frame. My father-in-law found it at a garage sale, and the person selling it wanted twenty dollars. He talked them down to one dollar and paid for his new treasure. It was my job to carry it out to the truck.

We pulled away from the curb and my curiosity got the best of me. I spoke up, "I studied it and I don't think I have ever seen anything like it before?" There was a pause, "Well, it's a table top saddle rack." "Oh, OK," I said as if I knew what he was talking about. "What are you going to do with it," I asked. There was a much longer pause. "Well, I guess I'll sell it in the next garage sale." He paused, "I could hardly not buy it after I got 'em down to a dollar."

I think about that story every time I drive by an antique store or a First Monday. But, oh my, how much stuff I have just because I got a good deal on it. It's very easy to save so much and get such good deals that I end up broke. After all, I might need it someday!

This came to mind at a church building committee one night, a group of six that had been carefully crafted and formed. They listened to others and took to heart what was said about what was needed in a church building. They struggled deeply to meet the requests, and I can tell you there were not ANY saddle racks in their plans. They tried desperately to accomplish this with CIF, as one put it. That is, cash in fist, but in the end they were about two hundred thousand dollars short, plus sweat equity. The committee filled in details at a Sunday lunch with steps and cost of each step.

Clearly, it was time to get the saddle racks out of the garages and attics and sell them. For the church members, it was a time to make a swap from homelessness to home, a time to complete the first phase of what started long ago. They all realized, as Paul puts it, "For we are God's servants, working together; you are God's field, God's building." (1 Corinthians 3:9 NRSV) They did not have to have a building to meet. However, it sure helps to have a place to greet new faces and welcome them into the Body of Christ.

Often we let our table top saddle racks deter us from accomplishing our goals. We have to clean them, sort them and keep track of them. What we really need to do is sell them. Instead of working in the garage this Sunday organizing your table top saddle racks find a church and be a part of a growing body. Come and receive the FREE gift of life. (Revelation 22:17) Be a part and give what you can. Saddle racks are accepted.

Old Becomes New

"Let me tell a story 'bout a man named Charlie" has a sound that has always stuck with me. Does it mean anything to you? The Kingston Trio first planted this song in my memory when they sang of protest and the rise in fare on the MTA (Metropolitan Transit Authority)[1]. I thought about them the other day as I went through my closet getting rid of shirts I no longer wear. The Kingston Trio always wore striped shirts. It reminded me of a study I participated in dealing with color preferences. The study revealed that people granted authority to men wearing pink shirts and the next strongest color was blue.

Blue conveys importance, confidence, intelligence, stability, and conservatism. It is interesting how we use the term blue in day-to-day conversations. If someone says, "I'm

---

[1]For more information see http://web.mit.edu/jdreed/www/t/charlie.html

feeling blue" we do not associate that with feeling smart or confident. We associate it with feeling sad. I noticed that when I am feeling pressured, tired or sad I tend to wear blue. It makes me feel better. So is blue up or down on the feeling meter?

Blue also reminds me of the saying one hears when someone is getting married, "Something old something new, something borrowed something blue" a phrase linking the past to the present. It shows hope for the future, the ability to count on friends, family and others with loyalty and stability. When I ask people what it means, most often the answer is, "I don't know. That's just the way it is."

It is difficult to understand when we do not know the tradition. Talking with a group, I asked what it meant to "turn the other cheek" and one person said, "It means I show them my backside cheeks and get out of there." Others thought it meant to live a passive life style. Walter Wink explains it as a means of peaceful resistance[2]. One thought, three answers.

When we talk to one another, we have to listen very carefully and ask questions to make sure that what we think we heard is the same thing that the other person thought they said. When we speak, it does not matter what we thought we said, what matters is what the listener thought we said. When we read the Bible, it is important to share and talk with one another to try to hear others' understandings of what is written. In those moments, we often feel the presence of the Holy Spirit as we hear something that was not said, but understood. You see the scriptures are not striped, not something to just get our interest. They are something old – yet something new. They are something borrowed and "True Blue". I hope you find something new, for you, today. Happy reading.

Is it Worth it?

It all seemed so simple. My computer was acting up, so I decided to replace one part. After the first part, I found two

---

[2]Walter Wink, *The Powers That Be : Theology for a New Millennium*, 1st ed. (New York: Doubleday, 1998).

others. After those, two more were found. I was wishing I had not started. Then I had to reinstall ALL my software. I was really wishing I had not started this project. I was being trapped one decision at a time. Do you know what I mean? I was down on myself for not leaving things alone. Several weeks have passed and I am grateful – things work much better. Looking back now, it was all worth it.

In 2000, Kathy and I decided it was time to quit secular work and respond to my calling to be a pastor. Over the seven years of training, I often asked, "Is it worth it?" I think I understand some of what Peter felt when he heard, "Get behind me Satan" or when he was sinking in the water or when he fell asleep in the garden. Peter may have thought this disciple stuff is hard work. Is it worth it?

Sometimes when I preach I feel full of the Holy Spirit. When I visit with others, I feel the closeness of God. When I write I am constantly amazed at what God does in my life. When I think about it, I know it is worth it. I still mess up and get covered up, but it's worth it.

Often, after giving our life to Christ, we wonder if we are doing the right thing. It is hard to see the good when swamped with details. We want to know how it will turn out when we are in the middle of the trip. We want to be able to turn to the last page and read the ending to see if it is worth the work to read the whole book. It is hard to wait without knowing what the end looks like. However, when we stop and take stock, we see life with God is awesome and it is worth it. Here's to looking back. The view is great!

Groundbreaking

It looked like a good day for some real fun time in the sand and the sun. Kids were playing and conversation was abuzz. Getting out where the air is fresh and the ground soft under feet is a time to relax and let your hair down. I wondered if any of the "grown-ups" were going to take their shoes off and wiggle their toes in the sand.

They began to gather, and words that had been blowing in the wind started to find homes in the crowd. Talk increased, each shared their excitement in what was a moment of suspense. What are they going to do? Am I supposed to do anything? I've never done this before. Then the words came out "Come on in closer so we can all hear."

Spades and shovels given to everyone and each person took a bag. The work was about to start. Welcome, welcome all, welcome to those that came far and to those who are good neighbors and to the faithful gathered here, welcome. The work was afoot with smiles on faces, and a glow about each person that showed happiness and joy.

It seemed like a simple process. Pray, pour and mix. Somehow, those simple steps transformed from a physical process into a spiritual event. Hearts lifted and joy found. Bags opened and dirt poured on the ground. Dirt that came from the founding church, dirt that came from the previous church home, dirt that came from the temporary church home and dirt that came from each person's home all mixed into the ground. This was more than a new home it had become a place where past and present were one.

One of the ministers, said, "I don't think I have seen so many different kinds of dirt in one place." All different types of dirt mixed and tilled into the ground by the eleven members of the building committee. It was to the glory of God that a new church was born, in a new place, with a new spirit. It was a new spirit yet it remembered the route traveled and the resting spots of the past.

As I looked across the other ten with shovels, I watched as they carefully tilled in each person's dirt. They took care and worked in fellowship and love with each individual. As I watched, I thought about the eleven disciples at Pentecost. (Acts 2) Each disciple focused on those gathered there. Each disciple took care and worked in fellowship and love with each individual so that they heard the Gospel in their own tongue.

People had come from all around and so had we. People came from diverse backgrounds and with diverse heritage, and so had we. I thought about the great meal shared and wondered about the meal that the first church shared. My mouth is watering already. Can you image the spread? Foods from every nation in all styles, it would be a new experience for a weary traveler. Three thousand saved that day! A new church planted and its strength is in its diversity.

Everyone brings something different to the table. Each one of us brought a bag of dirt from home. Yet we are all one in God because of the gift of Jesus the Christ, we symbolized this when we mixed our dirt together. Go ahead, have fun, wiggle your toes in the sand, shout into the wind, celebrate the groundbreaking discovery in your life. Celebrate your past knowing that God has made you for this moment. Hear the good news, Christ died for you. Come and join us at the table. It's a big, big spread.

The Rose of Attention

I sat there, coffee in hand, peering out the window. It was fall, and everything looked soft and comfortable, like looking through a camera covered with a silk stocking. The pecan tree was yellow/brown/orange and starkly contrasted against the green of the live oak. The two trees held hands and towered over my red tractor parked beneath.

My eyes moved closer and I noticed the green and brown grass covering the ground that provided a backdrop to see the green pipe fence just outside the window. Almost blended in with the trees and grass I noticed the rose bush in front of the fence. Yesterday, it seemed bare and now it majestically displayed a yellow blossom. The whole picture was reminiscent of a Monet painting.

I remembered Kathy saying, "When I get back to Texas I want you to buy me a yellow rose." There it was in our front yard, without any effort on my part. Had it not been for the rose, my thoughts of Arkansas would not have come to mind. The whole scene was relaxing, drawing me away from my plans for the day. The whole of my being was floating in the past. I could hear the rush of water bubbling along Clear Creek. I could feel the freshness of water as it danced across rocks. I felt the carefree life of a stick floating down the creek riding the ripples. All this came to mind in that moment.

My toast popped up in the toaster jerking me back in the room. Focusing on the rose wrought thoughts of the primrose path, a path to destruction. How easy it is to travel. The book of Judges gives a history of the Israelites sinking away from God and into the hands of captors. It must have been an easy path to follow, at first giving thanks to God for God's provisions. Then feeling they were doing all the work, finally forgetting about God completely. Once away from God, it was easy to fall into temptation and slavery. They would cry out to God and God would send them a savior redeemer. Names like Gideon, Deborah, Ehud, Othniel and on down the line until God gave us Jesus, our Redeemer.

It was not that anything I looked at was bad. In fact, it was all good and all part of creation. It was what I was doing with it. How often do we let our troubles, stresses and the world pull us away from God. We forget God's presence and need a reminder. God always seems to send us a rose to get our attention. If we miss the beauty, we feel the thorn. When we fall off track, we just need to get up, dust off and get back on track. God gave us Jesus to tell us it is okay. Jesus says, "Wake up and get back in life." I thanked God for that moment with the rose and turned my attention back to the events of the day.

What can Music do?

I was in the checkout line at the store the other day humming a little tune, which for the life of me, I can't remember now. Anyway, one of the people said, "I haven't heard that in eons." Another said, "I'm going to have that stuck in my head all day." It's strange what music can do to us and the memories that come with a few notes.

Somehow, our brain remembers things better when we put notes with it, possibly because it forces us to use both sides of our brain. When we least expect it, something will happen and trigger a memory which is often connected to a song. For example, if you are a football fan, you might walk by a TV in a store and hear a group cheering. The group may be on the *Price is Right,* but what you remember is a football game. Your head filled with stomping feet, clapping hands and the words, "We will, we will, rock you" puts you in a stadium. You can see the players on the field and feel the excitement and anticipation of a touchdown. Can you feel the brush of cold air on your cheek and the vibration of the bleachers? Can you see people standing up with their hands in the air and sitting down as the wave goes around the stadium? Can you taste the hot dogs and nachos?

Music makes things stick. Sometimes more than I desire. Whenever I hear someone speak of "hope," I see and hear the Seven Dwarfs singing "Hi Ho, Hi Ho It's off to work we go." Walt Disney made this famous in an animated film *Snow White and the Seven Dwarfs*. I didn't grow up watching the movie or singing the song. Why is this memory stuck in my mind?

It all goes back to raising children; I would like to think this anyway. One day we were on our way to church and I sang this little jingle.

I hope, I hope
So off to church I go.
Read Bible there and say my prayers
I hope, I hope.

I never intended to remember it. I can't even tell you why I made it up. Now when I hear the word "hope" I don't think "Hi Ho" I see my family driving in our old Suburban down Main Street on the way to church singing "off to church I go." How things come around in life is interesting. As a pastor, when I go off to work – I am going to church. Therefore, the merging of the two lyrics has come true in my life, off to church is my work where life is filled with hope.

We hope for so many things in life. Sometimes hope becomes so common that we dilute our hope in Christ. We forget the hope we have in church and the love that surrounds us as members of the Body of Christ. Yet, little things can joggle our memory. Just a song, a scripture or a prayer, hummed, said or thought anywhere. Once again, we feel God's love surrounding us and lifting our burdens. Our spirit restored gives us life. What do you feel when you hear the words, "Amazing Grace."

What is on Your List

Life would be so much easier if I did not have to figure it out. I need a set of rules so I do n't have to think about it – I can just live. Each morning I could get up and there on the table would be the list for the day. I can see it in my mind. Get up, put on blue jeans, plaid shirt and white socks – go to kitchen, pour milk, take meds, get out a bowl …. Clearly, it would have to be a detailed list, no decisions, just actions. At the bottom of the list, it would say, "From God."

I could do that and be perfect. God would be in charge and I could do what God desires of me. If anyone had a question about what I was doing, I could just hand them a copy of my list. But, would I be alive? On the other hand, I could concentrate on, *"Don't worry, be Happy."*

I was sharing with my son one Sunday all the things I wanted to do around the yard that would make me happy. He said, "Well you better get busy. According to Neil Sperry you should have finished last week." Neil should have talked with God and put it on my to do list, or God should have highlighted it because I didn't get any of it done. Now I am in distress. I am worried and that makes me un-happy.

I feel like the writer of Ecclesiastes, "For everything there is a season, and a time for every matter under heaven: …" (Ecclesiastes 3:1 NRSV) Where is that list? I hope I didn't miss anything. Oh, there it is. "Go and make disciples … Go, tell … Repentance and forgiveness of sins is to be proclaimed … Follow me. … Let anyone who wishes take the water of life as a gift. (Matthew 28:19 NIV, Mark 16:7 NRSV, Luke 24:47 NRSV, John 21:22 NRSV, Revelation 22:17 NRSV) Hum, no timetable. I think I can go and tell and give out water. Yes, I can do that! We can do that together. Don't worry, be happy. Our list is very clear.

How Much Information is Enough

We sometimes make decisions or set expectations with very little information. I would like to say "information we need" but "need" is a very confusing word. What one person needs is often different from what another person needs in order to decide. I thought about this one Monday morning when I went to the doctor. I arrived about 15 minutes early, signed the register and sat down.

I looked around for something to read and noticed that there was not a magazine in sight. What I saw on the table was about ten novels. Not small books the thickness of your finger, but books that were the same size as a Bible. I also noticed that I was the only person in the room without a beard and mustache. This is going to be a long wait, I thought, giving how long it takes me to grow a beard. Hum, it seems I am making decisions about time based on another's looks.

How much information is enough information? It is like the boy walking down the beach who asked someone to hold his money while he swam. He needed to know if they were a Christian and if they read their Bible and prayed before he would trust them. How much information is enough?

Expectations of time and money are the ones that bother us the most. I have heard said, a good manager is one that can make decisions and set expectations with little information. How do you feel about that? We are fine when we are setting what we expect of others but want specifics about expectations placed on us. We, as Christians, struggle with unspecified expectations. We want to know, "Who is my neighbor?" (Luke 10:29 NRSV)

The disciples asked if the time is now. Jesus replies that it is not up to us to know the time. (Acts 1:6) We want expectations set for us, we want them revised and with details. We want to know who, what, when and where. What we have is to work and wait until he comes. The Lord has trusted us to hold His money and only asked, "Will you hold it?"

Yet you struggle. "Give me something," you ask. "Cease to do evil, learn to do good; seek justice, rescue the oppressed, defend the orphan, plead for the widow." (Isaiah 1:16b-17 NRSV) That is enough for now. It is time to decide.

What's in a Smile

It's interesting to look back at my life and see all the different positions in which I worked and the experiences gleaned. I am amazed at the events that unfolded to create each one and I have felt blessed from each job. One of those jobs took me to Euless, Texas and I heard a sermon by Dr. Lewis Shambeck. He told a story about an older woman in a church. The story went this way:

> I went to help a church and when I arrived, I met an older woman in the back of the church, in the foyer. She shook my hand and smiled real big but didn't say a word. When church was over and I was on my way out, there she was again in the foyer. She shook my hand, smiled and didn't say a word. I met with the staff of the church and the board and we went over everyone's job and looked at ways to help them. I talked to everyone except this older woman. I turned and asked, "Ma'am, What is your job." She said, "My job is to smile them in and smile them out."

Later, I went on a business trip to Florida and took my family. We stopped in Perry, Florida at Deal's Famous

Oyster House to eat. When we walked through the door a little bell rang and the woman behind the counter looked at us, smiled, and said, "The best people in the world just walked through that door." It made us feel good and the food taste just a little better.

I applied that technology when I worked with doctor's offices. I trained people working reception, appointments and billing to greet people with a smile. I taught them, you could tell when someone is smiling even on a telephone call. When they call to make an appointment, you start the healing process with just a smile. To the receptionist and billing clerk, I said, "You are the first and last person a patient will encounter and you set the mood for how they feel about their health care visit."

Setting the context for an encounter is important to the outcome of the encounter. One time Jesus came to Peter on the lakeshore. Jesus met Peter on his own turf and helped him with his labor. Then Jesus invited him to a meal. He asked Peter, "Do you love me", and Peter said, "Lord, you know all things; you know that I love you." (John 21:17 NIV) Jesus said, "Then feed my sheep." It is a command for all of us to follow. Feed my sheep. We ask, how do we do that? What is it that Jesus is asking us to do? I think some of the ways we feed Jesus' sheep is to – meet people where they are in life, help them in their labor, smile them in, smile them out, and remind them they are the most important people in the world. ☺ I am smiling for you today!

I Am ALWAYS Right

It seems like cars are getting quieter and quieter these days. Sometimes they are so quiet we miss important information. I was driving on the interstate the other day in pouring rain. I slowed down and started to follow a truck in front of me. The windshield wipers were beating rain off the windows in what seemed like blade breaking speed. Yet they were failing at their job, and a coat of water remained on my windshield, making it difficult to see.

I slowed down and could see traffic barreling up behind me. I thought, I can either speed up – or all those trucks are going to give me a real rough ride. I sped up and moved my head closer to the windshield, as if it would allow me to see. With the beating of the wipers and the rain on the roof sounding more like a solid than a liquid, I could not hear the engine run. All of a sudden, I could feel the car slow down, yet I had not taken my foot from the accelerator pedal. I looked down and noticed the speedometer said 60 miles per hour. The car was running so smooth I did not feel it hydroplane. The wheels were spinning. I reduced the pressure on the gas pedal and felt the tires slow down and drop back down to the pavement.

About that time, the first truck whooshed by, and there was more water coming up from the pavement than was falling from the sky. The truck passed so close, it sucked my car toward it. I corrected my steering and gave a quick short burst of gas to maintain control. Then slowed down and moved closer to the shoulder of the road. I wondered how all the people flying by me could see.

I remembered back when I drove a truck. What I did was keep the taillights of the truck in front of me in sight. We drove through fog, sleet and rain placing all our confidence in the driver of the truck in front and their taillights. I got the feeling that the traffic passing me was doing the same thing I used to do. I did not think it was right.

It is a lot easier to condemn other people when they are doing something we are guilty of doing. We can readily recognize our own failure in others, even though we may not be aware that we have the same fault. We consider it different when we do it. After all, we know what we are doing. It is almost as if we are jealous that they are doing it and we are not. Maybe, it is our desire to control. Or, maybe it is feelings of anger because we did not give them approval to do what they are doing.

Jesus sent the twelve out with power and authority. On their own, they could do things their way. I think they may have gotten a little puffed up. After the transfiguration, the disciples could not heal a little boy and Jesus had to do it. Then they started to argue which of them was the greatest. Then John reported they saw someone casting out demons in Jesus name, and it was not one of them, so they tried to stop him. Just a little power, control, and it went to their heads. What was it that caused a failure to heal? Then they wanted to destroy a town because the town did not accept them. They have feelings of superiority and retaliation, far from the teachings of Jesus. Yet, Jesus did not give up on them. He sent them out again, seventy (two) in all, and they returned in joy after their service. (Luke 9)

I admit I was trying to follow the lights on the truck in front of me, but I could not keep up and my car hydroplaned. I responded poorly to those that were staying up. Like the disciples, I know Jesus will send me out again and I will return with joy. Now, I wait in anticipation to see what Jesus will do with me. How about you? Are you waiting with anticipation?

What is Really Important

Casting Lots

The church needed to make a decision, and many, many people got involved in the process. It was exciting to watch the church at work. People shared their personal experiences and their hopes. There were different opinions, but one church, varied ideas but one voice. All shared in love and respect for one another. In the end, the board chair made a tiebreaker decision.

During the early days of the church, or "The Way" as it was called then, we find several decisions recorded in the book of Acts. In the first chapter, we find that there were about one hundred and twenty in the group of believers, or ten people for each Apostle. Judas was now missing and they wanted to replace him. Somehow, they came up with two names. I wonder if they had discovery meetings and spiritual assessments. They prayed, "Lord, you know everyone's heart. Show us ..." Then Matthias was chosen by lot. (Acts 1:23-26 NRSV)

The next Sunday, church started by acknowledging God and telling the story of our relationship to God through music. It began "Lord of all creation" you know our heart "reveal your heart to [us]" "Lord there is none like you" what "Amazing grace" you have. So "Change [our] heart Oh God" let us be as one group chosen by you. Lord "Times are troubled, people grieve ... Hear our prayer". But we know that your "presence ... is in this place" and we will "trust you alone." Like the disciples, the church cast lots with their voices and hearts. The disciples, after casting lots, went out to do the work of the church. After worship, the church goes out to do the work of the church and serve God's creation. Sometimes, serving God is just a simple choice. How is your lot cast?

Responding in the Face of Fear

I love to go for walks in the mall, a store, out in the country, or even walking up and down my driveway. I see things I had not noticed before. Small things, like a new ant bed mounded to get out of water after a rain, or new blades of grass seeking the sun and popping up through the old dead blanket of previously mowed grass, a hawk sitting on top of the power pole, or the clouds floating by with gracious grandeur, gets my attention. Being aware of a wonderful world that will not stand still motivates me to walk. The world is moving and so must I.

It was on one of these walks that it happened. It was along a road next to a lake with large homes and lush lawns. Out of the corner of my eye, I spotted two Dobermans. They were running side-by-side in stride and step with graceful stretches that was a thing of beauty. I might regress at this point and let you know that I have a scar across the right side of my face where a Pit Bull attacked me when I was a child. I learned early on not to fear a dog barking, but to steer clear of a dog in silence. It taught me to have respect for dogs and I add -- wolves. The Dobermans were not barking.

When they were a few feet short of our position, their teeth came out and a deep growl came from both. I stepped between the dogs and the rest of the group of which I was a part. Raised my hand and pointed at the house and with all the energy I could muster I yelled, "Get back up to that house, now GIT." They turned and ran back home. Where did that come from, I thought. For me, it was an act of faith. I felt called at that moment to step out. Uncertain, unsure and with trepidation, I responded.

Life as a Christian is like that. Everything is just flowing along like usual, and then you see or hear something: a grimace, groan or sadness in someone's eyes. You know you have been called. Shadrach and the boys were just taking care of business when they heard the call. They stepped out believing that God would save them but fully prepared to die if God did not save them from the furnace. (Daniel 3:16-18) Being called is not about living, dying or knowing what to do, it's about believing and having faith. Faith is about stepping out of the boat when you cannot swim. Faith is about not being certain of the outcome. Faith is about moving when creation moves because creation moved. Faith is about responding when called. What is calling you in God's world?

Preoccupation

Distractions often block our vision and dull our lives. For example the story goes, suppose there was a man named Sam who liked to walk and enjoy creation. Sam shut the gate, locked it and off he went. If that goat gets out and eats the flowers again, my goose is cooked, he thought. He could not get the lock out of his mind. He had walked through the neighborhood and finally reached the edge of the woods when he remembered the extra bolt he always stuck in the lock. A fresh fragrance was in the air, but Sam did not notice. He was already a mile from the house. Three times a week he took this walk and today was especially important, but all he could think about was that bolt.

How could I have been so blind as to not put the bolt in the lock? I've got to get back, he thought, as he rounded the corner and started down the path through the woods. He picked up his pace, looking down at his feet. I sure don't want to stumble. He focused on each step moving one foot in front of the other faster and faster. The trail took him deep into the woods, where sounds are muffled and the air is cool and fresh.

He was so preoccupied with going faster he didn't notice the deer grazing in the meadow. The deer stood frozen as Sam marched by. He went down the path and out into the circle next to Mary's place. Sam was so preoccupied that he didn't notice the smell of cherry pies she had sitting out to cool. It was the very reason he walked this path. The first Tuesday of each month, Mary made fifteen pies for the homeless mission in town. Sam donated $100 to the mission each month so that he felt better about eating with them. It was the only way to get a piece of Mary's pie. But, Sam missed it all. His mind was on the bolt. Did he put it in the hole or leave it on the brick?

He rounded the last corner and peered down the street straining his eyes to see the gate. Was it open? He couldn't tell. Almost in a run, he could feel his heart pounding. Now it was painful yet he pushed on. He had to see if the gate was closed or if the goat was out again. At last, he reached the mailbox and turned up the driveway. He could see the gate now. It was shut and the bolt firmly in place. Well, he thought, as he slowed his pace, allowing his heart to catch up. His breath eased up a bit and he felt the tension leave his body. I don't know if I can continue these walks if they are going to be this hard on my health. These things are supposed to be healthy.

Jesus came so that we might "HAVE" eternal life. (John 3:16) Not just in the future, but now. What things in your life keep you from recognizing the fragrance of creation, the presence of God? The kingdom of God has come near. Repent and believe. Don't let unimportant things keep you away. The flowers will grow back if the goats get out. Go on, go out and take a walk. The dishes can wait and the grass will still grow, so you don't really have to stay and mow. Go have a little talk with God and let God open your eyes and heart to a wonderful creation.

To God be the Glory

Time sure flies when you're having fun. I felt like the church gave me a good report card one year on my anniversary. I felt successful about my part in the church. We all need to hear that we are doing well every now and then.

When I was younger, I spent a lot of time doing farm work. Each summer I would spend two or more weeks working on a dairy farm. I had two uncles that milked cows for a living, and I learned my way around the ends of things. Then, after high school, I spent two years doing contract farm work. I hauled and bailed hay, plowed fields, harvested wheat and oats, and spread fertilizer. At the end of each day there were always things left undone. My job was never finished, I never "caught up".

Later in life during my days of management, it was about making lists. Each day started with things left undone from the day before. If I was not careful, all I saw was what was not done, and that can be depressing. I started to balance depressing thoughts by making lists of things I accomplished or completed. Then I realized that checking things off a list had become the most important thing in my life. I stopped making lists. Lists were replaced by how I felt at the end and beginning of a day. If I looked forward to each day, the day was good.

A simple song reflects that style of life. "Count your blessings, name them one by one. Count your blessings. See what God has done." At the end of each day, I count my blessings. At the beginning of each day, I start with excitement because I cannot wait to see what God will do. I see blessings in smiles and in tears. I see blessings when pain is acknowledged. I see blessings when people talk. I see blessings when bread is broken in friendship and care. I see blessings in creation revealed. Count your blessings and "Give God the glory. Great things He has done".

Peering into the Atom

"Like the last pieces of a giant jigsaw puzzle, the final components of the titanic Large Hadron Collider (LHC) experiments at CERN are slotting into place,"[1] read the article. LHC, ATLAS, CMS, ALICE, LHCb initials thrown around

---

[1] CERN, *The last pieces of the puzzle*, 2008, http://public.web.cern.ch/Public/en/Spotlight/SpotlightLastPuzzle-en.html

in the discussion about the largest particle accelerator ever. Acronyms tend to make things hard to understand until you learn the lingo. The LHC will accelerate two particle beams to 99.9% of the speed of light. That is almost 670,000,000 miles per hour, or about 1½ seconds from the moon to our eyes.

What will they find when they peer inside, I thought? I reflected a moment to put things in perspective. A bullwhip first broke the sound barrier and then it was 1900 years before humans traveled faster than the speed of sound. We lived close to a military base, and growing up I heard sonic booms quite often. In school, we learned about seeing atoms and how they were composed. It was all about protons, neutrons and electrons. Now we look inside atoms. I can remember comparing an atom to our solar system. When I thought about God, I thought about our solar systems as the atoms that made up God. Our earth seemed to shrink in space.

It sure made God big and me very small. I cannot feel or recognize atoms within my body, so I wondered how God could know anything about me. I felt distant from God, and my problems so insignificant. Where is this God of the universe, I wondered? I felt like the psalmist "my soul yearns, even faints, for the courts of the LORD." (Psalm 84:2 NRSV) I dreamed of climbing a beanstalk so that I could see God's house and feel significant.

Then I read that my very hairs were numbered. (Matthew 10:30) Can you imagine -- A God that knows me so well that my hairs are numbered? Wow talk about peering in – God knows each hair! Even though I have many less today, I feel more loved and closer to God. Next time you feel lonely, lost or afraid try and count your hair. Then remember that God has already numbered them and probably the atoms in each follicle. Peering at things near the speed of light is here now; traveling that fast may come quicker than we think. We can know that no matter how fast or slow we travel, God will not lose track of our hair.

How do you picture God?

Don't Touch that Handle

It had been a great weekend. Joe, our son, came out to see us and brought a gift. Now Kathy has a new dog, Dexter. Dexter is a small dog that loves to run and catch Frisbees in the air, licks your skin and clothes. He has become our resident guard. Kathy had been thinking about Dexter coming out to stay for weeks. It was one of those "I want to, but I don't want to" deals. We wanted a dog, but we were not sure we were ready for the responsibility, especially a small hyperactive dog requiring lots of playtime.

Sunday afternoon, Joe loaded up his stuff to go home and as he was just about to get in the car, when he placed his hand on the door, and he stopped, turned and looked. I could see he was mentally going over a list. I wondered if he was reconsidering Dexter. He looked at me and said, "I learned that from Aunt Susan. Well, actually, she was teaching it to John and I overheard her say, 'When you put your hand on the door, stop, think. Have I done everything? Gotten everything? Am I ready to go?'"

Joe told us how much that moment has changed the way he does things. Every door handle he touches causes a reflection. He taught it to his employees. Before they lock the safe, they stop and mentally go down their checklist and see if they have forgotten anything. Joe said, "Sometimes, I can see them closing the door to the safe and they will stop and look around to see if I am watching. That's okay. They stopped and it gives them time to think. It has really helped at the store."

What I really like is the idea that when your hand touches a handle you should pause and reflect. You mentally run your checklist: is the coffee pot off, are the lights out, is the dog fed, do I have what I need, and have I given thanks to God. When Susan shared with John, she had no expectation that her words would be overheard and affect people in another city. We don't realize the influence our words and emotions can have on others and how far from the spot of expression they can travel.

Each time we reach for a door handle, a drawer handle, the filing cabinet, the telephone or the keys to our car, we need to pause and "be joyful always, pray continually; giving thanks in all circumstances, for this is God's will for you in Christ Jesus." (1 Thessalonians 5:16) Maybe you are not sure you want to stop and pray. You may have thought about it for a long time but you're not sure you want the responsibility. It is sure to change your life and it may change lives of people you do not know if you take that moment. If you are pausing and turn to see if I am watching, know that God is watching and listening for you and it's OK.

Flying off the Handle

When my boys were growing up, I told them stories that I labeled *Truisms*. I overheard a friend repeat one of the stories and he made the comment, "Oh, that's a Davidism." Truism or Davidism I can't say for sure, it is something I inherited.

---

[2] Sketch by Kathy Mays

Dr. Lewis Shambeck told a joke in one of his sermons and it reminded me of my summers in Pickton, Texas. Pickton is where many things were taught about life and how life goes on. I decided to take the joke and create a parable about life based on Pickton. This is one of those "if it ain't true it ought to be" parables.

You see, my aunt, when I asked questions, would respond with something like "That's the way things are" or "That's just the way it is." Everything that happened could be related to some fundamental truth. They lived a good distance from town and we would travel to the store and stock up every now and then. With this information, the parable became:

My aunt Alma could always find the truth and a lesson in everything that happened. I mean, one day we were sitting in the kitchen eating lunch. We had baloney sandwiches and a soda pop. Now, mind you, we had been slicing on that five-pound block of baloney for over a week and it was starting to turn (spoil), so aunt Alma threw the last hunk of it out into the yard between the house and the milk barn. That way one of the dogs, cats or other assorted animals could eat it.

Now, out back of the house, next to the milk barn was a corral and next to the fence was a watering trough. A huge hand crank water pump sat next to the trough. I had to climb up on the fence and jump on the handle to get it to pump.

I was sitting at the table looking out the screen door at that piece of baloney and I noticed a few buzzards had been circling the house. Buzzards like to sit together on things that are dead – like dead trees, fence posts, and telephone poles. Eventually they landed on the handle of that old water pump.

One of the buzzards flew down, got a hunk of meat, and flew back up to the pump and ate it down. It must have been full because directly it flew out across the yard, as if it was flying away and about the time it got between the house and the barn it dropped dead in the yard. I watched the second buzzard do the same thing.

I asked Aunt Alma to come and watch what was going on. She came over and sat at the table to watch with me.

Sure'nuf the third buzzard repeated the process. I looked over at Aunt Alma and said, "Now tell me, what the lesson it that!" She said, "Easy David, don't go flying off the handle when you are full of baloney." I had been had. She was right. Quite often, we get half pieces of information or make up our mind without thinking or processing. We don't want to hear the facts, our mind is made up. Then we fly off the handle.

James and John asked Jesus if they could sit at his right and left when Jesus came into his glory. (Mark 10:35f) They didn't have all the facts. The other disciples heard James and John ask and they got angry. They didn't have all the facts. Jesus called them together and told them a basic truth about life. If you want to be great, become a servant to all. You might say it's a Jesusism. How do I interpret following Jesusisms? Listen to all that is said: ponder on the words, feelings and emotions shared, then with a servant's heart engage in conversation and action.

Momma Mays' Rolls

Giving things time; time to grow, time to know, time to get accustomed, time to understand most things take time. During my business life, I heard things like "Strike while the iron is hot" and "The early bird gets the worm." This often translated into haste. Hasty decisions are wasteful decision. The old saying is, "Haste makes waste".

Kathy and I have always tried to give decisions time. When we made spot decisions, they were generally wrong decisions. It's like buying something off of the checkout isle merchandise shelf. You see it – it looks neat or your eyes think it is good for the stomach – and you buy it. Later, you find that you didn't really want the pounds that came with the flavor. It spoiled your appetite for the lunch you planned. If it was a book or magazine, it often ends up as trash in the car or set down next to a chair until thrown away.

I experienced enough wasted things in my life. Each time we moved, it seemed there were more and more things to pack and I could not ever remember using the items. So much so that now every time I feel pressure to buy, I don't.

That translates to – sometimes I miss good deals. Then as one of my friends puts it, "You can save yourself to the poor house!" We have to give things time and not make hasty decisions.

I first encountered giving things time as a young boy staying with my grandmother. Everyone called her Louisa Ann Spangler Mays, but to me she was Momma Mays. Momma Mays made the best rolls that existed. Her rolls were better than going to the State Fair and getting cotton candy. One of Momma Mays' hot rolls was bigger than your hand and melted in your mouth.

When Momma Mays made rolls, it took time. She would mix up some stuff and then let it sit. To me it was hours but in reality only forty-five minutes or so. Then she would mix some more and put the wad on a dough board where she would work it. How you work with something is important, she would say. It gives you time to think. "How long do you push on it gran'ma", I would ask. "You'll know when the time is right. Just knead it until it feels good."

Then she would pinch off three small pieces and put them in each section of a muffin pan. The waiting was not over. She would cover the pan with a damp kitchen towel and set them on top of the oven. We would wait. Slowly, we could see them rise. Those little pieces in the bottom would rise to touch the towel. That was the signal. When the rolls touched the towel, they were ready.

She would put them in the oven, so the wait was not really over. The rolls would continue to rise. Back then, there was not a window in the oven door. Everything was done by time and smell. The reward for waiting with Momma Mays was to get one, two or ... before everyone else got to the house. I can still taste them.

We have to give things time. We need time to let the Holy Spirit work in our lives so we can tell the difference between our desires and God's desires. How long should you wait, you ask. You will know – there will be signs. We have to check to make sure they are not fabricated signs. Elijah prayed and went to sleep under the broom tree. An angel woke him up and immediately he ate and went back to sleep. Later, the angel came back and he ate and traveled forty days. He must have eaten some of Momma Mays' rolls to go forty days. Then he had to wait in a cave, wait through wind, earthquake and fire before he heard the still voice of God. (1 Kings 19:4-13) God is here with us if we will pray, wait and listen. I wish I had one of Momma Mays' rolls while I am waiting!

Got Plans?

It was a long time ago, a time when I was young, energetic and imaginative. It seemed that all the males on both sides of my family had served in the military, and now it was my turn. I reflected on this during the long flight from San Francisco to Anchorage and on to Saigon. Why was I going to Vietnam? I knew I was going to serve my country, yet what were my personal goals in this matter. What did I plan on accomplishing? After considerable debate, between "me, myself and I", I determined that I was going to make a difference. I wanted to save lives. Yes, that is why I was going. I settled back in the seat with a new vision, and my angst greatly reduced. I was able to focus on the job and put the worry behind me.

My mission and goals have changed over the years. I am no longer young, but I am still energetic and imaginative. My vision in life is to discover God's plans for me and follow those plans. My mission is still to save all the lives I can. To accomplish my mission, my plan was to be a pastor in a local congregation. The first year of service as a pastor, I faced three suicide interventions. That was very unusual according to my mentor. I saw this as a confirmation from God that I was on the right track.

Later, at another church, we had vacation bible school (VBS) during the summer. There was a clearly defined vision with goals. We had a mission to perform. It made it easy to weed out the unnecessary things and focus on the necessary ones. The whole church came together with a common focus on VBS. Wow, was it great! The church was able to see that they could accomplish great things with a clearly defined plan.

We all need to stop every now and then and ask, "What is my purpose." When we answer that question, we can formulate a vision and mission to accomplish that purpose. Vision, mission and goals are three items required for a successful outcome. God's plans for us, "For surely I know the plans I have for you, says the Lord, plans for your welfare and not for harm, to give you a future with hope." (Jeremiah 29:11 NRSV) You can accomplish great things in your life when you focus on your purpose. We can clear out the clutter; reduce our angst, knowing that God has plans for a future with hope. You can make it happen because you can do all things through Christ, which strengthens you. (Philippians 4:13) Keep your vision before you, your mission clear, and your goals reasonable, and you will find a future in hope.

Building Community

Many of us remember our days in high school when we built our first set of friends. We ran around together, met at the DQ, the malt shop, dances or anywhere else two happened to stop and others started to gather. It was our first attempt at building community outside of home, church and school. Some people hold that first community for a lifetime. The rest of us have started over and over building community.

Many look back to that early style of community with hearts yearning for a home and family with a similar experience. Sadly, most of us were unable to hold on to our first community. It starts with some going off to college and the group gets smaller. It happened when people left town for jobs. It happened when we sent our friends off to war, some of those do not come back at all, and some come back different. Community seems to change and evolve as life progresses.

One of the things I have noticed about strong communities seems to be the regularity that they meet and share meals. It seems that community is more about quality than longevity. The more meals shared, the closer the community. Personal guards seem to drop and allow others in –

to the deeper self. Community is trusting to the point of vulnerability, to be hurt if necessary.

Many are willing to give their lives for freedom, but few are willing to give their life for community? We have this built in protection of privacy. I wonder why we can go to war for community and sacrifice career, family and finances, but not willing to give up those same things for community.

As families grow, it becomes more difficult to maintain community. In the Hebrew Bible, the Old Testament, I read about all the "convocations" in Leviticus. I recognize them as community builders. Offerings brought were cooked and shared, a time of community at the table. God established these gatherings as a time of joy and prayer. (Isaiah 56:7) By the time Jesus came, they had become a duty and a business. Free will offerings became taxes, gifts of food became money of convenience. Jesus rejected this evolution driving them out of the Temple. (Matthew 21:15).

They had stopped giving of themselves for community. It takes work and sacrifice of a few to build and maintain community for all. When the church does not give of itself to make this happen, business and profiteering are ready and willing to take over. Community is lost to capitalism. Everything tied to profit, not sharing.

When Jesus called Peter at the seashore, Jesus asked of Peter, "Feed my sheep". (John 21:15) This was both figuratively and literally. Jesus was asking Peter to build and maintain community. Most important for us to notice, it was not a command. It was a request. A request filled out of love, not duty. "Peter do you love me?" "Then feed my sheep."

Christ calls to us today, "Do you love me?" If we answer yes, then we must be willing to be one of the few to become vulnerable so that we can build and maintain community, not because we have to, but because we love Jesus. All who will come and join at the table is community. Anywhere two stop and gather we build community. "For where two or three are gathered in my name, I am there among them. (Matthew 18:20 NRSV)

Do you "know" a community? What are you willing to give to keep it alive and viable?

Watermelons

We are at the end of another watermelon season, so I will have to do without until next year. I don't think I will forget, as a child, watermelon juice running down my chin and onto my stomach. I was a sticky wet mess with the biggest smile from ear to ear. Uncle Bascom grew the best Black Diamond watermelons you could ever taste. Bascom never sold a melon. He gave them all away. You might wonder what kind of person acts that way.

There was a time the banks were short on funds. The bank in Winnsboro sold all of its assets to the bank in Sulphur Springs and then went broke. Bascom had all his money and loans on his trucks at the bank in Winnsboro. The bank was one of two left in the country without FDIC insurance. He lost all his money and still owed for his trucks. I don't know how he felt inside, but on the outside he forgave and went on. When the bank president in Winnsboro died, Bascom was the first there to help the widow. He survived and built a new business only to face the threats of an organization that wanted him to join or be shut down. He didn't join and he survived.

I feel sure he was not the only one that experienced things like that in East Texas. I was not old enough to be included on how everything happened. What I remember is a community that stayed together, helped one another and expected nothing in return. It was a community that gave out of their needs not excess and it taught me to be a Christian.

We hear news of stock markets falling and prices rising. In such times before, Christians came together and through prayer, fasting and faith found ways to persevere. Times like these are times people turn to faith. The church must be ready to help the lost, afraid and without. Paul's instructions to Timothy were to remind the rich to not be arrogant but to be rich in good deeds, generous and willing to share. (1 Timothy 6:17-19)

Everyone has something to give even if your 401K is bust and you cannot fill your gas tank. You have your hope, your scraps, your seeds to plant and at least one rock for rock soup. Maybe, plant a watermelon vine. You might consider a once a month fellowship which becomes once a week or once a day. You may eat beans, stew and cornbread, the deer population may decrease and you may learn to fish. However, your faith, fellowship and trust in a God that loves you should not diminish. When times are tough, begin to think of ways to help those who suffer from a financial crash or hardship. What can you do without, to help others?

Colorado

Half Moon Campground

Sauerkraut, sauerkraut, even the name tells me I shouldn't put it in my body. When I was a kid, it sounded like sour krout (sic). I didn't know what krout was and I didn't want any. I especially didn't want any that was sour. It had to be worse that buttermilk. Buttermilk didn't taste like butter at all. Popeye may have liked spinach, but that wasn't enough to make me like it!

Sauerkraut fell into one of those categories of foods I ate so I could have dessert. That was the rule at our house. If you cleaned your plate, you got dessert and I always wanted dessert. I liked mom's lemon pies the best. Next was chocolate and least was rice pudding. All desserts were worth putting up with a few unsavory vegetables. Like those tiny little heads of lettuce boiled with bacon, or the green things that looked like miniature stacks of wheat bound and standing in a field. Mom would steam, salt and butter them, but it didn't help.

When I no longer lived at home, I stopped eating "those" foods. There was no more: sauerkraut, brussels sprout, spinach, cauliflower, cabbage or broccoli just to name a few things that went off my list of acceptable foods. Celery was okay. I could take a stick of celery and use it like a knife to scrape peanut butter from a jar. I ate celery not because I liked it, but once I put something on my plate I needed to eat it.

I think it was 1977 we were camping up the road from Half-moon campground alongside the creek. We had a long day of mountain travel, and everyone was tired. It was dark and cold, so we huddled around the campfire. Somebody put something in foil over the fire. In a few minutes, they passed it around for us all to eat. I was so hungry I didn't care that I couldn't see what was in the foil. Hum, tasted pretty good. The next morning at breakfast I asked, "What did we eat last night?" "Cabbage", came the reply. Cabbage! I can't believe I liked cabbage!

That was the first of a long line of discoveries in eating vegetables. It floored me the first time the words came out of my mouth, "I think I'll have a vegetable plate." What a change, what a transformation. As children, we learn many things that are good for us but often rebel and refuse when we are free to choose. When I started college, I laid off reading the Old Testament. Maybe reading the Bible is one of those things you have chosen to leave off.

I also left off anything that was remotely related to opera. One Christmas, our choir director decided we would sing the *Messiah*. Like I said, I was not interested in that "opera stuff" and the *Messiah* sounded like it might be opera. The director had a good tenor voice and he opened the music with "Comfort ye, Comfort ye my people, saith your God." (Isaiah 40:1 KJV) I was not really in gear to hear what it said but it felt good hearing the words. The rhythm was good and it felt comfortable. I was comforted.

Maybe I might just read that book of Isaiah. Often we need to hear and experience things anew and from different perspectives. Then we discover it was not what we thought. Our mind opens and we receive a blessing. Would you like a bite of fire steamed cabbage, try Revelation 22:17.

Alpine Tunnel

While living in Longview, Texas each evening, with the sun at my back, I exited the freeway onto Alpine Road. The road sign sparks a reflection of a journey made to Alpine

Tunnel years before. I was on my way to Tin Cup, an old ghost town between Gunnison and Buena Vista, Colorado. After passing Pitkin I saw a sign that read Alpine Tunnel 10 Miles. I decided to take a look. The road started at about 9,655 feet and was a gentle slope up through the trees with many stopping points that captivated my interest.

Just over 11,000 feet the road, as I know roads, stopped. Travel began on an old narrow gauge roadbed. It felt like hanging on the side of the mountain bumping over old crossties. There was no room to pass, and the road must be checked to see if it was clear before starting a section, or it was a long way to back out! It was difficult slow travel.

The views and country were wonderful, full of contrasting color of white, green and soft browns that drifted off into the west. I held great respect for the people who worked building the tunnel and track. They completed a great feat. They must have faced many fears working while hanging on the side of the mountain. Yet at every breath, beauty was all around them. I wondered how they paid attention to work details when the brush of cool air across the cheek invited a look out, to an awe inspiring sky.

Throughout our vacation, we encountered many trying places, yet at every breath we met new and wonderful people. The trip taught us to see the beauty of God's creation in people, places and events. It was a time of intrigue, wonder and discovery. Looking back on this trip, reminds me of Paul on his missionary journeys to spread the gospel. He traveled by ship and foot; our vacation was in a Chevy 4x4. Paul gained in wisdom and the ability to show people the wonder of God's creation as the journey progressed. I wonder if I helped anybody see God's creation during my vacation.

Paul was rejected run out of town starting in Damascus and it went downhill from there. However, when Paul met Lydia things changed. (Acts 16:14) Lydia accepted him and invited him home. I can see Lydia smiling at Paul and saying, "Paul, thank you for telling us about the scriptures. Can you stay awhile and tell us more?" Instead of confrontation in the Synagogue, Paul found a welcome home and listening ears. In the next town, Thessalonica, Jason took his place in jail. Paul experienced grace and by the time he spoke on Mars Hill Paul's message must have changed. Paul found a new way to share the Gospel. Paul traveled a bumpy road getting to Mars Hill yet wonders were at each breath.

Sometimes, we have to face our fears before we can walk in confidence. Paul found his confidence on Mars Hill when he pointed out the "unknown god". I discovered confidence driving mountain roads, traveling that narrow roadbed to Alpine Tunnel. After Mars Hill Paul changed, after Alpine Tunnel I changed. Experiencing a difficult journey allows us to recognize the blessings that God has provided all along. Then we can share them with others.

How have you shared God's presence in your life with others.

Courage in the Face of Adversity

[1]From the Red Mountains looking toward Silverton Colorado 1978.

I stood looking back towards town through my zoom lens. Was town to the right or the left? I wish I had a map. Storm clouds were all around and the road seemed to drop off the other side of the mountain. It had been hours since the last time I saw anyone. Where was I and which way was out? My first trip four wheeling with my family, in the mountains, was not going well.

What is it that makes us afraid? Are we insecure with who we are, apprehensive about something we need to accomplish? Does new information shake us? Do we feel desperate to have something in our lives? Do we lay awake at night tormented by thoughts about what happened in the day or what we think might happen tomorrow? Maybe we are hesitant to accept a job assignment or new responsibility. Do we get fidgety when put on the spot and asked to give our opinion? Are we alarmed when others turn to us for advice because we are unsure of ourselves?

All these are forms of being anxious. "The disciples saw him walking on the lake and they were terrified. "It's a ghost," they said, and cried out in fear." (Mathew 14:26 NIV) They were anxious for their lives. Can you remember a time in your life when you were scared? Can you relate to the disciples in the boat?

I remember sleeping in the open when my fear would creep up on me. It is somewhat like an old cowboy folklore story I read about at the Library of Congress. An old cowboy was asleep on his blanket. "About a half-hour before sun up next morning, I woke up and found a snake on my shirt bosom." "What in the world did you do?' Well I did the only sensible thing a person could do. I went back to sleep!'"[2]

The old cowboy experienced my fear. I wish I could say I would have gone back to sleep, but in my dreams that is not what I do. I think about throwing the covers over the snake and letting it have the bed. I know a rattlesnake is 100 times faster than I am and it would not work, yet it remains in my dreams.

When the disciples saw Jesus and felt afraid, Jesus replied, "Take courage! It is I. Don't be afraid." That is what the cowboy did, he was not afraid, he patiently waited

---

[2]Sanderson Nita Davis P.W., Terrell, "Rattlesnake on My Shirt Bosom," in *Folklore* (Terrell County District NO. 19: 1936).

working within God's creation. The next time you feel afraid or anxious, I hope you remember the words of the Old Cowboy and are able to remain calm assured that God loves you and will not abandon you. I pray that God will give you the courage to know God's presence and do whatever is the right thing to do in the moment. Calling out in the midst of our fears we hear, "Take courage! It is I. Don't be afraid."

Experiencing Something New

I love to explore things and places[3]. Most of my life I have spent two weeks every year in Colorado. Exploring and enjoying God's creation is always more fun when I am with friends. I have noticed that often what we set out to see is not what we end up enjoying.

One year, several families gathered at South Mineral Campground just west of Silverton, Colorado for camping, hiking, and four wheeling. We decided to take a hike up to Ice Lake to fish. Well, I should say, two of us wanted to fish and two wanted to watch. It was three and half miles up for a total of a seven mile hike. We started at 9,833 ft elevation

---
[3]Trail to Ice Lake, Carl Jacobs, Bill Hurlbut and Kathy Mays.

and the climb finishing about 12,300 ft. at the lake. It was the time of year where it freezes at night, rains every afternoon, and gets up to about 75 degrees in the heat of the day. It was a perfect time for hiking. We all thought we could make it.

Just short of 11,000 ft and several long hours into the trip, we came upon an abandoned campsite. There was a bear bag hanging in the tree, a tent with a pair of tennis shoes nicely placed beside the tent flap, sleeping bags and clothes inside with bear claw marks down the side of the tent. Needless to say, we didn't find anyone in camp. However, we all perked up our eyes and ears and reviewed bear procedures. We started to walk a little slower and the climb was a little rougher. In such an open country there seemed to be a shortage of air.

We popped out of the trees in Lower Ice Basin and found ourselves crossing two streams, one from Island Lake and the other from Ice Lake. The water was about waist deep and cold, cold, cold. We started to move much slower. All we could see above us was snow – deep snow. We had a quick discussion about why they might have named it, ICE LAKE. Maybe it was time to change our plans and return.

We chose to move to a lower lake and fish. We shared great joy, fellowship, food, and struggles with each other. For the four of us it will always be a memory. It was a great challenge for us that pushed us beyond our normal envelope. This push taught us we could do more than we expected and that joys came in challenge and strength came through adversity. We changed because we tried. We discovered that the trip was worth the effort. It was humbling yet spiritual. Because of our efforts, we all moved closer to God.

John Wesley left England and went to Georgia to tame the natives. He failed. On the return trip, he discovered he was not sure of his faith and felt he could not preach. His friend advised him to preach faith until he had faith. Later, Wesley recorded his unwilling presence at a Bible study in which his heart "was strangely warmed" and he knew he had faith. His struggle started with a trip to Georgia, a new thing for Wesley.

The trip to Ice Lake was a new thing for us. We didn't make it all the way up because we were not very well prepared. Like Wesley, we came back a little unsure about our next outing. Also like Wesley, the trip changed our lives. Wesley found faith being faithful, our faith increased because of our trip. Are we doing faithful things in our lives, are we "taking the trip" or are we just waiting for the destination?

Would you like to take the trip? Start with Bible study or worship; it might change your life? From Genesis to Revelation, you will find God. If you would like a small trip to start, I can assure you there are fish if you start with the Gospel of John. Take a chance it will be worth it.

Staying the Course

John Bunyan starts his book Pilgrim's Progress[5] with a poem that describes how he set out to write one book, but when he was close to the end, he discovered he had

---

[4]CR18 East of Ouray Colorado.
[5]John Bunyan and W. R. Owens, *The Pilgrim's Progress*, New ed. (Oxford [England] ; New York: Oxford University Press, 2003).

written something else. It seems that I often want to go one direction and end up going another. There are roadblocks, detours and chug holes. Sometimes an article starts with one thought and ends in another. A sermon will start one way when I plan it weeks or months in advance, and then change based on life events and reflection during writing.

Earlier in life, changing course would bother me. At a young age, terms like "strike while the iron is hot" and the "early bird gets the worm" were the word of the day. "Stay the course," my mother would tell me. I have tried to follow those instructions, and often I am not deterred to the right or the left. Yet I have come to learn that sometimes, original thought and beginning plans is not where God wants me. When I am determined to "Stay the course" a blessing may be missed.

We must keep ourselves open for new possibilities, new events and new creations. This can be a painful process. When I'm moving at full speed and hit a road block, it knocks me back. Through life, Kathy and I have discovered that snap decisions are wrong decisions. Like traveling too fast, snap decisions do not give time for reflection and consideration of alternatives and the full cost of a predetermined action. Prayer and a night to sleep on it usually shed light on what we did not consider. We need to give time to understand the Holy Spirit. We need to have a time to separate our wants and our desires so that God's desires might be revealed.

Jesus often went off to pray. He prayed all night before he selected the disciples (Luke 6:12) and he went to the garden to pray all night before he was arrested (Matthew 26:36ff). Jesus also stuck to the plan, but it was a plan made by God. Once we are sure of the course set before us, we do want to continue to stay the course, to be the early bird and to strike while the iron is hot. Yet, at each step, we should do careful reflection on the path taken. We check to see if our personal desires have taken the path in a direction *away* from God. I pray that you have steadfast prayer and careful reflection in your life today.

Finding Rest

Reflecting on an upcoming family vacation to Colorado, I remembered many trips from Fort Worth to Amarillo, across the bottom of Colorado to South Fork, up through Creede alongside the Rio Grande Reservoir to Stony Pass, my favorite place to reflect on life, creation and God.

While traveling, small towns along the way became a focus of our attention. Each trip we found different parks or playgrounds to visit. We made it a practice to stop every few hours and let everyone out of the car to rest from the ride. We would buy gas, drinks and snacks for those thirsty or hungry and find a city park, church or school playground to run off the restlessness of the boys. We would drink our drinks and play until tired. Then to the gas station for restroom breaks and back on the road, usually accompanied by a chorus of "On the Road Again" the way Willie sang it.

---

[6]Kathy and Chris Mays at the top of Stony Pass Colorado 1978.

Traveling on long highways reminds me of one of my favorite sayings: "What is the hardest job in the world? Resting, there's no way to take a break." Riding in a car can be very tiring, and to stop and take a rest requires activity, which to the body is rest. Rest is different things at different times. Rest takes on a different light once I reach spots such as Stony Pass. Stony Pass is the very beginning of the Rio Grande River.

I could sit at Stony Pass looking out to the east for hours, and rest. I have never gone alone, always with others. I wonder if God sat there on the Seventh Day and smiled at creation. Do you have places that allow you to calm down and find rejuvenation? Is it a place you go alone or with others? Sometimes it is restful to go back to the beginning. Not to start over but to observe what has taken place.

Jesus says, "Come to me, all you who are weary and burdened, and I will give you rest." (Mt 11:28 NIV) Gathering together as the Body of Christ is one way to find rest. I suggest at least three doses a week in fellowship with others. This is a way to rest from everyday burdens, a way to take a break. In these moments of busy rest, we encounter Jesus and find the rest and rejuvenation we seek. Invite friends for a meal, a movie, golfing or just to sit around and talk about nothing. All the while, you visit, be aware that somewhere in your midst Christ is restoring you to wholeness.

Christmas Sessions

Is it Fall or Autumn

One cool day well before Christmas, traveling down a back road of East Texas, I rounded a corner and there before me was the perfect burnt-orange tree. It must have been sixty feet tall and shaped like a candle flame burning in the stillness of air. The leaves were in symmetry and harmony with each other giving me a feeling of comfort. Several things seemed to fly through my thoughts.

The coolness of the air transported me to a time with my Dad. It was the time of year, we would go out into the woods with saws in hand to cut and gather a supply of wood for the winter. These trips, always accompanied with stories of the past, also gave a feeling of comfort, a feeling of belonging. The stories focused on a place in the surrounding area or in an area that was similar. They included times of struggle, times of joy and a few mischievous moments.

The comfort from that burnt orange tree provided a memory of a loved past and an anticipation of Christmas. Comfort ye, Comfort ye my people (Isaiah 41:1 KJV) floated through my memories of the *Messiah*. Reminding us that God is with us, cares for us and we are not alone.

So, I thought, was it fall or autumn? How we look at life reflects the words we choose to represent an event. Seasons give a flavor; they help set the stage of thought and memory. From childhood, I learned fall, winter, spring and summer. I wondered, why that specific order of words. Often we hear life events referred to by seasons. In the movie *Finding Forrester,* William Forrester writes a letter to Jamal Wallace. "Seasons change, young man, and while I may have waited until the winter of my life to see the things I've seen this past year, there is no doubt I would have waited too long had it not been for you." I wonder if my Dad discovered life anew as he shared his stories with me. I wonder if he thought it was the winter of his life?

For the character Forrester, the end of life is associated with winter. I struggle with that thought. Earthly life does not end in the winter. It ends in spring, a time of renewal, re-birth, a time of hope. Winter is a time of slowing down, a time to reflect and identify what is really important. Forrester meeting Wallace forced a reflection of events buried deep within and it took the spring of a relationship for him to recognize that value.

I think I prefer "Autumn" over the word "Fall". Fall is about leaves falling from trees and the starkness of life exposed to the harshness of winter, cold and chilling. If winter is the end of life then fall is the dying process. Autumn is about comfort and beauty. It is about the fullness of life and the expectation of change. It is about being part of a bigger picture. It is about feeding the earth in preparation for renewal. It is a time of rest and hope.

Paul describes God to the people of Lystra saying, "He has shown kindness by giving you rain from heaven and crops in their seasons; he provides you with plenty of food and fills your hearts with joy." (Acts 14:17 NIV) I like that explanation of God. God gives us crops in their seasons. One of the crops of autumn was a sixty foot burnt orange tree. Autumn crops, autumn color, autumn comfort, autumn hope gives us a joy and an expectation of renewal. It reinforces our hope of Easter and resurrection.

I think life is not four seasons, but many seasons. There are times that we feel the cold and we fail to see the beauty of winter. There are times we feel the punishing heat of summer and fail to see the beauty. There are times we feel drenched in the rains of spring and fail to see the beauty. When we say, "it's fall", we are looking at loses in life. I say, it's autumn and God is reminding us, "Comfort ye, Comfort ye my people!" Autumn is a time to remember. Rejoice and rekindle your hope that God is with us.

Anniversary

From our fifth Christmas to our twenty-fifth Christmas, Kathy and I spent our anniversary, December nineteenth, buying Christmas presents for our boys. Work, business, school, church and family matters seemed to allocate all hours and minutes of the day from Thanksgiving to Epiphany. The secular world of Hallmark and advertising took precedence over spiritual life. Well, maybe all my life.

Everything I did was something that gave joy to my heart, even exams at school! Yet everything seemed to be crowded out. Selecting presents for others and anticipating how they would react gave me joy. I yearned for time to accomplish giving. I liked watching children in the church parking lot ogling at the live nativity with lights highlighting shepherds, angels, wise men and Mary, Joseph and Jesus complete with music for their ears.

Each year I would get lost in the bustle and noise of Christmas. I would push to get more work finished; make a few more dollars push, push, push until I crashed. The crashes were never at the right time. When I crashed, I would reflect on what is important in life and why. For some reason, I seemed to always reflect on Elijah. Elijah pushed until he fell asleep under a broom tree and wanted it all to end. He slept two days and then traveled forty more in preparation to hear a whisper. (I Kings 19:4-13) During the last month of the year, I often felt like Elijah. My time was not my own, and it seemed everybody wanted something. I lost focus on what was important. I thought everyone was out to get me. What I needed was forty-two days to listen for God's whisper. I wonder if Jesus went to a mountainside by himself to pray so that he could hear a whisper. (Matthew 14:13)

It is important for each of us to stop our busy lives and give time to hear a whisper. I believe in a living God that still speaks. If I want to hear what God has to say, I have to allow time for listening. Silence is not optional. It is required. It requires silent alone time. I confess, sometimes I have to plan a trip to the mountains to find time alone in silence. Yet sometimes I can find it on a bench in the mall or at my desk chair after reading. I know I can find the place and time or I can wait for the wakeup call – the crash. My experience is that wakeup calls are not the preferred method of communication.

I hope I don't have to travel forty days and forty nights to hear God's whisper. During Advent this year, find time to listen for God. Prepare yourself for the arrival of the Christ child. Determine what is important in your life, and listen for the whisper.

Who took Baby Jesus

We left the house one Sunday to attend the Children's Christmas Service at church. There next to the barn at the end of the driveway was our Nativity display. We were very proud of our Nativity. Our sons hand-made the nativity set when they were young. Tim, the youngest, helped to paint under the supervision of John, the oldest. Ten years later, Tim contracted a rare cancer and died. That made the nativity very special to us. When we returned from church a few hours later, we discovered someone had taken Baby Jesus, the shepherd and the cow from the nativity. We were heartbroken; it was a very great loss.

Jesus was born in a barn in Bethlehem and eventually he would be stolen away. It was at night in the garden when they came and took him. Later, as Jesus was dying on the cross, he said, "Father, forgive them, for they do not know what they are doing." (Luke 23:34 NRSV) Jesus also said, "I pray also for those who will believe in me through their message." (John 17:20 NIV)

For the person(s) who took Baby Jesus that Sunday night, the prayer of Jesus holds true. "Father, forgive them." Most importantly, the nativity reminds us to forgive ourselves for past wrongs. Jesus was born, lived and died so that we might experience God's grace in our lives. God has forgiven you, you are forgiven, now forgive yourself. Forgiveness is the first step in recovery and restoration. Jesus came so that we might be restored to God.

Somewhere there is a new manger scene. In that manger scene, there is a part of my son. I pray for those who will believe when they see Baby Jesus. In a way, it will change the world. We all have the ability to change our world. It is our choice if the change will be for good or bad. Our actions and our thoughts affect how we treat others and how we view ourselves. Can you pray "Father forgive…"

God knew what the outcome would be and still chose to send Jesus. May we all experience forgiveness of our failures because of God's grace. From the cow, we can know that all creation recognizes God's gift to us. The Shepherd reminds us there are people here that will help us find the way. The Baby reminds us that it is not the powerful, but the humble that find mercy. May your thoughts and actions today be for good and not bad.

Christmas Pud

Kathy, my wife, came in the room and said, "You'll never guess what someone gave you today?" After thirty-eight years of marriage, all questions have become fun, so I indulged her and started guessing. I really stretched to pick some weird answers. All of them only seemed to intensify the joy in her eyes. Her smile would get bigger, her eyes more blue and she would shake her head, NO. What could it be, I thought. Finally, I said, "I think you're going to have to tell me, I don't think I'm going to get it."

Well she said, "You know I have a friend at work?" Yes, I nodded. "Well her husband's mother is from England and she made you a gift, something very special." Well at least I know whom my gift was from, but what was it? Why would she give a gift to me? It would be Christmas in a few days. I could wait to find out.

We gathered at my son's house with all our extended family. There was great joy in seeing everyone and hearing updates. We gathered around the table and shared a meal. At the end of the meal, Kathy brought out the surprise gift. It was Christmas pudding. A dap of sauce was placed on my slice of pudding, and I slipped my spoon down through the mixture and into my mouth. Flavors began to burst in my mouth as eyes beheld a fireworks display. Sweetness settled upon my tongue, and memories came forth from times past like flavors bursting from the Christmas pudding.

    I remembered times past watching people take their first bite of Christmas pudding, the look on their face and the sharing of the experience. I remembered mother in her apron, making sure everyone that wanted to try Christmas pudding had an opportunity. I could hear the kettle shrill and the hot water pop as it poured into the pot. I could remember family and friends, the good times and sad times. I took the last bite with tears in my eyes. Truly, the flavors of time had come to me and joy flooded my heart.

    Thinking about the moment of that bite, I wonder what Peter and Paul remembered when they took bread, broke it and drank from the cup after Jesus' death and resurrection. When Paul participated in the Eucharist, he might have seen flashes of light and heard the voice of Christ. He may have felt the hands of Ananias and experienced restoration of sight. Likewise, Peter might have felt water under his feet, sounds of the cockcrow or words from Christ, "Do you love me?" I can only imagine what they experienced.

    As I savored that bite of Christmas pudding, I remembered my mother, my family, friends and I said, "Yes, mom, I love you." I remembered Kathy's friend's mother-in-law who did not know me, but through an act of agape love gave me a gift. When I take the bread and drink the cup during communion, I remember the gift of Christ and say, "Yes, Lord, I love you." I remember all those who have loved and cared for me. It is in simple acts of agape love that we find peace and wholeness in the Body of Christ. What memories are special to you?

The Book of Color

I remember a book that fit in my hand. It went from the tip of my fingers all the way to my wrist. I looked for it every year; it was my favorite thing at Christmas. Now, I am not talking about a book that you read. It had striped colors that reminded me of a rainbow, and it only opened to one spot. When opened up wide, I could see through the cellophane on both sides and the treats contained within. My eyes would get big, and a smile would come on my face. It was time to choose – which would be first? There were assorted, cherry, butterscotch, and others. My favorites were cherry and butterscotch. The book always came in a stocking with an orange, apple and banana. I am talking about a book of Lifesavers©.

Each year, in my heart, I still experience the joy of receiving my stocking and I get a big smile on my face. One year there was a change in me when I was more excited about what I had given others than what I might receive. In fact, I changed so much over the next few years that I really didn't want anything for Christmas except to give something to others. I realized that giving was something I received as a gift, a gift from God. Giving became more important in my life than anything else did. Life became not what I wanted or had, but what I could give.

Once I had a spirit of giving, I noticed a twist about some requests people had about giving. Some said give to the church so that you might receive more, it was giving to be blessed, like buying a prayer cloth so your prayers would be answered. Then all I could think about was Matthew 12:38-44 and Luke 20:45ff, where Jesus taught the disciples how the teachers of the law would devour widows houses to make themselves look better, they would even take a widows last two cents. It made me hesitant to talk about giving.

For me, giving is not about how much the church has or doesn't have or how much the church might need to make ends meet. The church is God's church, and if we don't give, then God will get it from dry bones. The church will find a way to survive just like the disciples survived going out without a purse or bag. We give to the church because God has given us a gift. When we give, it makes us feel complete. We give because it frees our hearts and lifts our spirits. It can put a big smile on our face and heart.

This Christmas, as you scurry about looking for special gifts or think about what you might receive, remember the rainbow of lifesavers. Remember God's covenant sealed with the rainbow. We are in a relationship with God and we give because giving makes us feel complete. We give because we need to give. What reasons do you have for giving to others?

Lent

The Trailer

Home was in an eight by twenty-four foot trailer six months one year. Many asked, "How are you getting along". Mostly my responses kidded about my situation. "It's not much to clean," "I can get from one end to the other in a few steps." After a month or so, the trailer was relocated from one end of the campground to the other. After the move, the awning and one of the beds was un-folded. With the extra space, there was no more sleeping on the couch and there was room to stretch out. It is interesting how fast I adjust to new surroundings.

Like many, I think I am a flexible, adaptive person. However, we, as humans, like things the way they are. We resist change, and like to have routines even when we deny we have routines. It is not until something forces a change that we realize that we were in a routine. Change gives us an opportunity to evaluate ourselves. I had become accustomed to a small space and was unsure what to do with my newfound space, even though it was still small. The change gave me a chance to evaluate how I adapt.

Lenten session gives us a similar opportunity to evaluate our life and surroundings. In preparation for Easter, many will give up something for Lent maybe a food or activity. Several things can come from such an action. One, we can find out if we may be addicted to what we have given up. Two, it gives us time to focus on Christ and the Christ event.

"No one can serve two masters; for [we] will either hate the one and love the other, or be devoted to the one and despise the other. You cannot serve God and wealth." (Matthew 6:24 NRSV) If we have an addiction to anything, we are trying to split our loyalties. Asking ourselves how we feel about what we are missing will give us a clue. For example, if you gave up sugar for lent and everything is just not sweet enough, you may be addicted to sugar. One hundred years ago, people didn't eat more sugar than salt. Can you imagine that! Chocolate did not have sugar in it at all and it was a health food.

The important thing is that when we skip a meal, don't eat a specific food or whatever we have chosen for Lent, not only should we evaluate its affect on us, we should replace the time with thoughts of Christ. It will not take us long to discover where our loyalties lie. We ask, are we thinking of Christ or thinking about what we gave up. Once our thoughts focus on Christ, the old things can be a part of our lives again as long as they take the place of something other than Christ. Hopefully, we will get to the point that Christ is first and everything else comes as a part of Christ so that "everything [is] by prayer and supplication with thanksgiving." (Philippians 4:6 NRSV) This is a goal in our relationship with Christ.

I discovered during the time in a trailer, I had become addicted to space and things. I missed my television, my library, my seemingly endless supply of coffee and popcorn. All those were things that caused me to think about them instead of God. Now that I have experienced being without and returned to my home, I give thanks when I get in my layback chair and turn on the television with my bowl of popcorn. I do it after giving thanks to God.

Getting the Lint out of Lent

Momma Mays made a wonderfully warm quilt that I liked to use when I took my afternoon naps. She made the quilt from old snuff sacks. I wonder if it was the smell or the feel I liked about that old blanket. I did not know about the snuff sacks until years later, after my introduction to the quilt, so I doubt I will ever figure it out. Momma Mays also made blankets from old shirts and other things. I guess if you have nine boys, two girls and you're a sharecropper, you make do with lots of things.

Some of that has rubbed off on me and I tend to look at everything to see if there is any possibility that I can use it. Sometimes I end up saving things that I must later throw away, but it does not deter my spirit to search for use in discarded items. I have had limited success with lint that comes from the dryer. When I clean the lint screen, I am very careful to roll it up from the bottom – the bulkiest part of the lint. I end up with a tubular shape, which I press to make a flat mess that looks like a sponge. I use it to wipe up the washer and dryer, and then I throw it away.

Getting rid of things does not come easy for me. Sometimes there is a desire to save that piece of lint for next time. Lent is a most difficult time. I never want to give up anything. My blanket could not go on a shelf for forty days. I could be coerced to give up something like lint. Especially if it meant I did not have to wash the clothes. Besides, giving up lint for Lent had a ring to it, something I could remember. I tried giving up chocolate, and a few times coffee. Most of the time, I do not give up anything that makes a real difference. I guess I leave the lint in Lent.

Giving up something for Lent should not be just doing without something for a short period. When we give something up for Lent, we should use the time to focus on the things we need to change in our lives and to prepare ourselves for Jesus' death and resurrection. Lent is a time set aside for spiritual preparation, a forty-day period before Easter. Giving up something for Lent should cause us to remember to spend time in prayer and reflection.

With that in mind, I sometimes add something for Lent. Therefore, my daily routine increased. It was something that really needed doing or it forced me to remember to take time to think. Setting aside time to wrap up in a warm blanket so that I could remember Momma Mays, family, good times and God's love helped me to focus on the lint in my life. Taking time slowed me down and unblocked my vision of who God wanted me to be. It seems what we need most is to get the lint out of Lent and focus on God. It may mean doing without and it may mean wrapping up in a warm blanket of sacred love. How do you prepare for Christ?

Changing Times

Dexter

Have you noticed how difficult – difficult things are to do? Dexter, our dog, is a mixed Australian Shepherd and Miniature Pincher. He is black and white and looks like a tiny Holstein cow. He loves to herd things: cows, dogs, cats and people. Anything that moves, he is ready to herd. He can run and jump, catch Frisbees in the air and has what seems to be no end of energy.

Dexter does not like to be alone. He wants someone around at all times. It was good for Dexter to come to our house because we have over three acres for him to run and play. However, for him to run and play requires someone to be there to interact with him.

Several months ago, Dexter met a friend. Dexter's friend had other dogs and cows. Dexter decided that he was better off at the friend's house. I suppose because he could keep the cows herded. However, the friend's house did not need one more dog, even if he brought the cows to their front door every evening and kept them there.

Reluctantly, we put him in a small fenced area in the back yard. We could tell Dexter was sad for a few days. Then he decided we had created a new game. We put him in the fence and he found a way out. My son started calling Dexter Houdini because he was so good at getting out of his fenced back yard. He would get out of the fence and then stand in the front yard and bark at the other dogs trying to get them to come out and play.

Dexter came home from my son's home, but not to a fenced area. Dexter became a dog-on-a-wire. We set up a wire run in the back yard that gave him a 120 by 50 foot area to run. He tried to get loose by chewing the wire, shaking the halter off, rubbing the clip loose and breaking free with force. None worked. I know after a period he will succumb and give up. I wish it didn't have to be that way. I wish he would stay home because he wants to stay home, not because I put him on a wire. We cannot let him continue to herd the cows to the front door at someone else's house, so he must be restricted.

Often, in our lives, we find ourselves like Dexter. Regardless of training, regardless of constraints, we decide we want to do something else and nothing will deter us. We are oblivious to the fact that we are causing problems in other areas. We think the cows and people are happy when the cows are at the front door. We continue to accomplish our goal by any means necessary and expect a reward for our ingenuity and efforts. That is, until we find ourselves on a wire. Then we ask, "God why are you letting this happen to me?"

Throughout the Hebrew Bible, the people would be off the wire and on the wire. They struggled with the fact that they were the light to the world and not the "gift to the world." God never abandoned them and continued to encourage them. Sometimes I feel like Dexter, expecting a reward for herding people instead of shining a light. I find myself on a wire and I wonder why, yet knowing God's encouragement creates energy and excitement about what can be if I will but listen.

A New Way

Have you experienced a time when someone would say something, triggering a distant memory that really seemed to come from nowhere? The other day I was in a discussion and someone said, "Google it. That's my answer to everything, just Google it." The distant parts of my mind went back to the seventh grade, standing in the front room of the house calling out to mom, "Hey mom, how do you spell, xylophone." "Look it up in the dictionary," was her reply.

"Look it up in the dictionary," I thought. If I could look it up in the dictionary, I would know how to spell it. All a dictionary can do is confirm that I spelled it right or wrong. How can I find it – if I can't spell it! My struggles were always in English, never problems with things like ASA, SAS, SSS or any of those terms.

A recent trip on my computer to Google with "zylaphone" gave the immediate reply, "Did you mean: top 2 results shown." He was right, just Google it. However, ASA, SAS and SSS did not yield the correct results on Google. For SSS the first entry was, . Interesting site, I thought, the Selective Service System. I haven't thought about that for years – many years!

Well, maybe my poor English skills Google can help. I am glad I "got" Algebra because Goggle didn't help that at all. Adding Algebra to the search of SSS didn't help. Adding Triangle to the mix finally returned results that would help. It seems that to find information we must be careful how we structure our questions.

When I go to the dictionary and look for a word, I sympathize with the disciples. Jesus tells them about the leased vineyard, they get the wrong answer and Jesus says, "Have you never read in the scriptures." (Matthew 21:42

NRSV) A few verses later, he tells them again they do not know the scriptures. Which one, 1 Kings, Jeremiah, or Isaiah it seems they were doomed to fail. After all, they did not have Google back then. I doubt they had an index as well!

The same difficulty comes to mind when I hear songs like, "I'm Using My Bible for a Road Map." What does that mean? Every time something happens in life, they just look it up in the Bible. There are tons of stories of the right way and the wrong way to use the Bible to find answers. Answers are there. We have to figure out the right question to ask.

"How do you find something in the Bible," I would ask mom. "Well," she would say, "Your Dad always said, 'You ask someone.' And if they don't know the answer they will ask someone. Then when someone asks you, you will know it has been around the whole church." We, the Body of Christ, become the Dictionary, the Google, for life. Got problems, pray, read and talk with the Body of Christ. Keep asking until a solution is found.

The answer may seem to come from nowhere. "Fear God, and keep his commandments; for that is the whole duty of everyone." (Ecclesiastes 12:13 NRSV) What does that mean, you ask? "You shall love the Lord your God with all your heart, and with all your soul, and with all your strength, and with all your mind; and your neighbor as yourself." (Luke 10:27 NRSV)

Waiting in Line

Have you ever noticed people standing in line? Some stand with eyes looking front, not to the left or to the right. Some keep their eyes focused on the floor, unwilling to make eye contact with anybody. Some focus on the person checking at the register or look over each item purchased by the person in front of them. Some read all the candy bar wrappers and magazine covers. I guess I have been all those persons at one time or another. Waiting in line gives me time to think about life.

However, you might be able to tell that what I like to do best is watch and talk to people. Yes, I like having a captive audience stuck in line waiting their turn. I watch faces and body actions to events that transpire. Once with four or five in line at the grocery store someone rolled up a full basket joining the person at the cash register checking out. It more than doubled the wait time for all those standing in line. Conversation and time seemed to stop. Those waiting looked intently at the person and basket entering their line. How do you feel if someone breaks in line in front of you? How do you feel when someone breaks in line behind you? Are you even aware of what goes on in line behind you? Many people "bite their lip", they think they are not saying anything, but they might as well speak because their feelings are written on their face.

If I am waiting in line and someone comes to join me, my preference is for me to move to the back of the line and join him or her. I see that action as a courtesy to the others in line. Once Kathy and I had been in line for a long time and I had to leave the line to visit the necessary room. When I returned to take my place, I felt bad. I thought everyone was looking at me being a "line breaker". Is there such a thing as saving one's place in line?

Later, we were at the grocery store with about fifteen people in line. They opened up a new register next to us and we moved to that spot with about five people in tow. I turned and said, "Look you only have a few items why don't you go before us." I did that with all five persons. Four of the five had difficulty going first. Did they feel they were breaking in line? Did they have trouble taking a gift from another person? It seems we all have different sets of values and become uncomfortable when something happens outside our norm.

Different intrinsic values cause us the most angst. We somehow expect others to behave based on our values, and when they do not, we are hesitant to discuss the differences. We prefer instead to pass judgment on their actions and condemn them to wrongdoing. The early church struggled with this as well. One of the great questions was, "Do you have to be Jewish to be Christian?"

Paul wrote, "Let us therefore make every effort to do what leads to peace and to mutual edification." (Romans

14:19 NIV) "Do not cause anyone to stumble." (1 Corinthians 10:32 NIV) We stumble trying to decide if we can live by someone else's rules if only for a moment. Is it about rules or is it about dialogue. Are we afraid to say what we are thinking? Maybe our fear is based on our lack of experience in speaking with a stranger. We pray, we ask, we observe, we accept others, and at the top of the list, we talk to one another and work it out in a way that leads to peace and mutual edification. Step right up; it would please me if you go before me in line.

Pecking for Freedom

There certainly seemed to be a lot of sickness going around. If sickness were the result of sin, I think we would all be in a lot of trouble. There are good things and bad things about being sick. When I am sick, frozen sherbet seems to make me feel better. It coats my throat and calms my stomach and it tastes good. I can sleep late and everyone is okay with my tardiness. In other words, when I am sick I get away with many things, so much for the good part of being sick. When I am sick, I cannot go and visit anyone. I have to stay home. Therefore, the worse thing about being sick is that it isolates me.

Isolation is never fun. We can feel isolated even when healthy. When in a room full of people, at a family reunion, shopping, or at a church gathering it is easy to feel alone. When our views are not accepted or recognized, we feel isolated. When angry or afraid, we feel left out or isolated. Isolation tends to form a protective shell that is very difficult to break and it seems to thicken and harden as time passes. It grows without notice and becomes totally encompassing. We allow the process to continue as a protective measure to keep us from getting hurt. How can we thaw from our frozen isolation?

Living in a protective shell is a strange concept. It's like getting sick in order to sleep late. It might work, but there are side effects. Shells may protect us, but they also enclose us. We become the ember removed from the fire. Isolation makes us cold and hard. Suddenly, we find ourselves trapped in our own protection.

When I find myself wrapped up in a shell, I don't like to think about it as an egg shell but I do. For a chick to escape, they must peck from the inside. That means I have a responsibility to act. When I am shelled up, I want someone else to come to comfort and encourage me. Freedom from my shell may be a few pecks away, but when choosing to sit and wait for someone else to break me out, I may end up scrambled. Therefore, if I want out, I must be a participant in the process.

Very few people discovered God by sitting at home shelled up. There are accounts of God calling people sitting at home. However, it seems that most people finding The Christ were out seeking something. How does one seek to find The Christ? We are seeking when we help someone else. We are seeking when we meet with the Body of Christ. We are seeking when we take any action that is not self-centered. When we seek, we are pecking.

Peck, peck, peck is our way to discover Jesus. When we discover Jesus, we peck to encourage others to peck. Don't get shelled up. Keep pecking for freedom.

Finding the Truth

One night I sat listening to Tchaikovsky's 1812 Overture by Erich Kunzel and the Cincinnati Pops Orchestra with the volume turned up enough that I could feel the music. It brought back memories of the first time I went to the Dallas Music Hall. Mom thought it was important to expose me to things outside my normal daily life. Things like chocolate ants, liver and onions, and classical music. In my opinion, they were things I didn't need in my life!

I can still remember when she said, "David, we are going to hear the orchestra play at the Dallas Music Hall! Aren't you excited?" Yeah, excited. That is not exactly what I was thinking. I remember entering the hall and feeling cold. It was the middle of summer and we did not have air conditioning at home so it was a strange feeling, like going into a deep dark cave.

I settled back in my chair and listened at all the noise coming from the stage. I kept thinking it would sound better if they would play together. I didn't know they were warming up, tuning their instruments. The conductor finally came out on the stage, the "real" music started and it sounded BORING. A lone cello played and I slid down in my seat and thought, well at least I can get some sleep if it was not so cold in here. I heard drums playing. That's not so bad. Then it went back to violins and I was back asleep. I thought about the music I heard on the radio and in my head started singing along. Then things started to change.

Something I had heard before, it sounded like a storm. Now I knew why it was so cold in here. Have I really heard this before, I thought, as the music died down to sounds of a butterfly flittering across the flowers. My eyes got heavy, I nodded and all of a sudden, from out of the silence charging trumpets blasted me out of my seat. It was the Lone Ranger! OK! – no one told me I was going to hear the Lone Ranger theme song. Maybe classical music is not so bad after all. After the William Tell Overture, we heard Tchaikovsky's 1812 Overture. That day at the concert caused my musical taste to widen.

When I listen to the 1812 Overture, I can feel the air around Moscow as Napoleon's Army advanced. Voices sound, as if in prayer, knowing the battle is coming. It seems they are saying, "Help us Lord as we face this moment. Give us strength. We have confidence in you. Yes, yes we can endure." Then a period of angst as they prepare and wait – anticipation builds. A few cannon shots ring announcing the conflict and people have fallen – some have died. In their minds they must think, "Why, am I here Lord, I am not sure, I'm scared."

We hear Tchaikovsky's 1812 Overture every year for the Fourth of July. We see fireworks and hear cannons. We all know how it turns out. Napoleon is defeated and Moscow stands. The musical score sounds out success. This is music to live by, music that can stir the soul and call us to action.

Had the music existed eighteen hundred years earlier, I think the Disciples would have played it on the way to Jerusalem on Palm Sunday. I can see the Disciples blowing smoke from the ends of their fingers as they entered town shooting down the "Bad guys" and ushering Jesus to his rightful throne. It all feels so right. However, that was probably not what Jesus was feeling, or was it? Jesus and the disciples may have experienced the same music, same crowd, yet had very different experiences.

When you hear the words, "Take up your Cross and follow me!" (Matthew 16:24) What do you feel? Do you feel a chill run down your spine and think, "It's cold in here, I'm scared, why am I here, help us Lord." Or, do you feel your fur and emotions rise as you think "yes, we can endure we can do this?" We can do everything through him who gives us strength. (Philippians 4:13) Christ is calling. Can you hear the trumpets and the cannons? Aren't you excited?

Lawn Mowers and Taxes

Well, it's that same time of year again, a season I both love and dislike. I love all the green, the flowers and I like doing yard work. Mowing is therapeutic. The problem is the rain. When I have a chance to mow, it rains, and I cannot mow in the rain. That forces the days I can work in the yard to be the days I do not have available. What time I have seems to slip through my fingers. When it dries and I can mow, it becomes a TASK. Pleasure and therapy is gone like the wind. It is also tax time.

Sometimes the rain and the tax reports tend to rain on my spirit. It's easy to get overwhelmed and slow down. Sometimes it gets so bad I have to remember to put one foot in front of the other. I lose my appetite and don't eat. Tinges of depression cover my soul, causing me to feel like a drowned rat.

I remember years of staying up all night, balancing books and filing tax returns often late at night on the day they are due. I would rush to the downtown post office in Fort Worth, where it was almost like a party. The postal employees would dress up like Uncle Sam and stand in the street with huge mailbags addressed to IRS Austin, TX. People were honking horns and waving at each other. It felt good to put it behind me, finished. The release of tension was as calming as floating down a river with my hook hanging out the back of the boat. Drifting along as the hook bounces over rocks, giving just enough tugs to keep me awake.

We let many things pile up in our lives that slow us down. Things like family, finances, guests, church functions and often relationships. One thing will tend to loom over all the rest. We feel that as long as that one thing is staring us in the face we cannot do anything. All progress stops. We wait on everything until that one thing is out of the way.

You might say we are facing a Goliath. Goliath stood nine feet tall and trapped all of Israel. The entire army was depressed because no one would go forth and fight the Philistine. (1 Sam 17:4-11). God sent a young man named David, who with one rock felled this giant. David used skills he had been taught and practiced, nothing special. David just put one foot in front of the other and finished the task at hand.

My son, Joe, calls this having God in our corner. When we feel overwhelmed, undervalued and stuck in our tracks, we can remember that God provided a savior for a hurting world over and over and over again. God will be there for you if you will allow it. God can give you the strength to put one foot in front of the other. Like David, we have been prepared for this moment. It doesn't take anything special, just what we already know.

A Perfect Mother

Normally, I do not compare myself to anyone. We need to compare ourselves to who we are capable of becoming, opening up our possibilities in a non-condemning evaluative manner. However, a friend sent me a story about Mother Jasmine. Jasmine is one of those mothers that smiles at everyone, loves all and refuses none. Jasmine is what a Christian should be: giving, open and non-judgmental. Jasmine is worth my time and effort to use as a comparison.

The first thing I noticed about Jasmine was that others did not need to be like her in order for her to care for them. In fact, you might say Jasmine is a one of a kind. Some examples; Jasmine accepted and cared for are: five fox cubs, four badger cubs, fifteen chicks, eight guinea pigs, two stray puppies, fifteen rabbits and one roe deer fawn. She loved, welcomed, warmed and helped them psychologically adapt, removing their stress.[1] Jasmine, found abandoned in a locked shed, was malnourished and abused. You may have guessed by now, Jasmine was a greyhound dog.[2] The key to Jasmine's love was that she gave without expecting anything in return. Jasmine is like Mother Teresa, easy to praise, hard to follow.

When God sent Jesus into our world, we locked Jesus up, beat him, belittled him and tried our best to kill him. Humanity reached out and attempted to kill and take power over the God that we claimed to love and upon whom we depend. We were unable to accomplish our goal, and in the face of our failure God responded by welcoming us, helping us, calming our fears.

Jasmine welcomed all new arrivals by sticking her nose in their cage and giving them a lick. God welcomed us by sending Jesus and the Holy Spirit. We can welcome others with a smile, a handshake, a hand up. We provide places of refuge and encouragement and give our money, time, resources and talents. Being a good Christian is like being a perfect mother.

What must we do you ask? Like the man seeking eternal life, we must shed those things that block us from God and others, pride, resentment, retaliation, judgment and chasing other gods. We must use our resources to help others and to follow Jesus the Christ, expecting nothing in return. It is a gift, a reflection of our love.

Graduation

May of each year I reflect back to my own graduations. It is my second graduation that really gets my attention. I had so much on my plate that I did not know I had graduated. Sounds strange, doesn't it? You see, I was working a full time job, a business that required trips out of town, I was active in

---

[1] http://www.dailymail.co.uk/news/article-1103645/Meet-Jasmine-rescue-dog-surrogate-mother-50th-time.html , accessed Sept 22, 2009

[2] http://www.all-creatures.org/stories/a-mother.html, accessed Sept 22, 2009

church, and there was family, including three boys at home. I completed my last college course between trips to Canada. Then it was Christmas, New Year, kids back to school and more trips out of town. I came home one weekend and my wife had thrown a surprise graduation party. Wow, I really passed, I thought.

I am sure that Kathy noticed there was not any free time in our schedule. I was so busy I could not see that I was covered up, stressed to the point I could not see the stress marks. Does this sound familiar? Have you been there? Sometimes, when I am at my best I am at my worst. When I am at my worst, I am at my best. Is the glass half-full or half empty? Is it filling up or emptying out? Am I an optimist, a pessimist or stressing out totally? I had so much that I had nothing.

I possessed things, scheduled things, and even got things done, yet, I could not enjoy things. At times, there was a longing for a simpler life with more time in between. The discovery of problems of plenty pounded my presence and pulverized my passions; provoking persistent resistance to change that must come if life was to continue. I was totally flexed out, stressed to the max.

I realized that angst was present more in times of plenty than in times of scarcity. It seems like a backward statement. I discovered that many of my problems were rooted in what to do with what I had. Life was easier, smoother, and calmer with less, and yet the drive was to acquire and do more. The rope pulled tighter and tighter closing me in, tying me down.

Maybe that is when I realized what Jesus was saying, "How hard it is for those who have wealth to enter the kingdom of God!" (Luke 18:24 NRSV) My desire to pursue points on earth and not points in Heaven was causing my angst. Like the young man Jesus spoke with, things were distracting me from the important ways of life. I remember twenty-four years after graduation filling a dumpster and the Goodwill dock with burdens off my back. It felt good to be free. I had finally achieved the graduation I so desperately needed. I got rid of what I had, so I could follow Jesus. (Matthew 10:21)

The Wooden Chair

It was a small wooden chair. I think a blond oak one. It sat next to the floor furnace in the front room. What I remember is two things about the chair. First, my mother was sitting in the chair when she told me I was going to have a brother, I was only five years old. The second thing I remember is sitting in the chair with my lower lip stuck out, my arms crossed, pouting and blocking all communication. Finding out about a new brother – only once; sitting in a pout – often.

Mom would leave me alone in the chair until I worked out what was bothering me. Sometimes my sister would fan my stuck out lower lip with her finger, causing me to make blubbering music with my sobs. I must have looked pitiful. I was resistant to changing my mood or my mind. It was a great personal challenge to choose if my arms would stay crossed, held tightly against my body, or if I would flail my arms wildly in the air to keep away my sister's finger. It did not seem to matter which I chose. Both would change my attitude. When my arms would fly out from my body, my sister would move, and it became a game. A game I would lose right along with my pout.

I do not remember if I was in the chair for punishment or if it was my choice spot when I was hurt or angry. I suspect it may have been some of both. The chair was my place to chill and get a new perspective. It was what I needed when I needed it. Today, when I am hurt, afraid, scared or angry I can still put on a "good pout". I no longer have the oak chair in the front room, but I still find ways to pout. I can go to the garage, sit at the computer, go for a walk, or get something to eat to name a few things. In reflection, I can see that pouting equals setting myself aside from the situation. Okay for a moment but not a place to stay.

When I withhold my presence from conversation or from participation, I am pouting. When I lash out at others or block what they are doing, I am flailing my arms. I hope that I am learning to make these times healthy and not detrimental. Often, my own desires caused the situation.

I wonder about the time James and John asked Jesus to let them sit on the right and left in his glory. Hearing no to their request, I wonder if they pouted. When the other ten disciples heard they wanted the best seats, did they get angry and pout. Jesus helped them discover their perspective. Do you want to be greatest then become servant. (Matthew 20:20-28, Mark 10:35-44) Wow, what would they do now? If I were in a pout I would think, "What good will that do!" My attitude would be flailing my arms accomplishing nothing. The act of serving causes us to stop blubbering, our arms return to normal, blood pressure comes down and reality comes back. Jesus provides what we need, when we need it.

How do you pout? What helps you get out of your pout? Remember, God loves you and is aware of your situation. God may let you pout for awhile. Then, God will come in, stir your heart and help you understand your perspective. It will be time to get up, become servant for all and once again be at one with God.

There's More To It

So packed full of events are some weeks that it is difficult to discern what was best. When this happens, it is often without warning or planning, and we recognize it only after most of the events are past and over. It is good to stop and review such periods so that we may plant retainable memories. Journaling or writing in a diary is a great benefit to help remember.

We were sitting in Strawn's Eat Shop Too on 70th Street in Shreveport one Sunday talking about the past week. Included in the conversation was the person waiting our table. He told of high school graduation and plans of college. When I asked what he enjoyed most about high school he replied, "Playing Lacrosse." He said he was looking forward to some time off from school. He left, and in the continuing conversation, we agreed there was more to it than was shared. We were all hopeful that he would go back to school. That started a whole new conversation about "more-tuit" and "round-tuit".

It seems there is always more to it that keeps me from getting around to it. Often when I finally get around to it I find that there is more to it than I thought. Do you know what I mean? Our imagination makes things different from reality. I suspect that when the young man gets to college he will find there is much more to it than he thought. If he is like me, after college he will look back and think there was not much to it. It all seems to pass by in a blur.

Conversation helps us to sort things out. When we tell someone else or listen to someone else's experience, it helps us to put things in order. We get a chance to see what was missing and what was possible. Conversation opens our eyes.

Rhoda, on hearing Peter's voice, got excited and ran to the others saying Peter is here, Peter is here. Yet it took dialogue, conversation, before the others got a-round-to-it and opened the door. Then Peter was able to tell them how much more-to-it they did not know. (Acts 12:12f) We have this information because many gathered at John Mark's home to pray and were in conversation with God. Eventually, many got round-to-it and wrote these things down so we now know there is more-to-it.

Betrayal

I was talking to Mom one day about birthdays. She handed me a book and said, "Look in here. It's all in there." I started to flip through the pages and stopped on a page where I found written, "Paul given 30 days to live." Deep inside I felt a pit in my stomach. Why wasn't I told that Dad only had 30 days to live? I would have rearranged my entire schedule; I would have spent more time with him. I would have asked some questions that I had always wanted to know.

We often find ourselves saying I wish I had done this or I wish I had done that or I wish such and such had or had not happened. When a new event happens in our lives we look back and think these things. Sometimes, looking back is like looking through a mirror and we get things backwards, confused or twisted. It is important for us to remember these "things" helped shape us into who we are now. The good, bad and indifferent all had a part.

Years after I read about Dad, I reflected back on that moment sitting on a bar stool in Mom's kitchen. Why didn't I complain? Why didn't I ask why I was not told? I thought about it for a moment and wondered if I was really listening. Maybe the pain was too great for the person telling me, and they softened the words so that I read past them and missed the point.

Often we say, "If only." If we are not careful we can "IF" ourselves into oblivion. Looking back can be helpful if we allow the question to inform us of the present. We must be willing to be critical of our own thoughts and actions and not look back to assign blame. We must be open to re-interpret what we believed to be true.

When I first read that page in the calendar, I felt betrayed and left out. After reflecting, I wondered if I had been too busy to hear, to eager to let soft words go by without clarification. I decided in the future I would pay more attention and not be bashful about getting clarification. I realized I need to feel confident enough to ask questions.

We ask of hardships, "How did I get through that period." Thinking and talking about such items will give us strength to persevere. Asking, "Why did I do that?" will give us wisdom. Figuring out why someone else did something may be a futile exercise, or it may give us understanding about that person and how we can be their friend. It may be self revelatory.

I wonder what Paul felt when he looked back at his life as Saul. Did he see Jesus one day and reject him before the Damascus road experience? I wonder what Peter thought when he looked back at the time he sank in the water or when he denied knowing Jesus. I don't know what they felt. I know they became powerful witnesses for God, telling about the gift given of Jesus the Christ. I know they had strength to persevere when times got tough and they didn't give up. They didn't give up when they were put in chains, threatened with death or thrown out of town. I pray that my experiences in life have prepared me for the challenges that lay ahead, whatever they may be. I hope I can ask questions, persevere and continue to be God's witness in God's creation.

The Call

As a boy of thirteen, I knew God had called me to share the Gospel and wondered, "What does that mean?" SMU, Southern Methodist University, sponsored an event for youth that felt called to serve the church. During the event, we toured the facility. The first stop was a room with a gigantic swimming pool. Thoughts of, "Okay, I can do this it's just like camp only bigger and indoors" came to mind. Then they led us to the student center – lots of people; it must be fun, I thought. Next was the lecture hall, boring! The library came next. No one will ever read all these books, besides why read history. Life is about the future, not the past!

All that I need is the Gospels, good Ol' Matthew, Mark, Luke and John. Relating to Jesus is all that is required. Can you hear Jesus complaining about phylacteries and Tassels? I'll spend my time doing and leave the reading to others. After all, God will inspire if needed to know.

Then Vietnam and conflict with "Thou Shall not Kill" and a job requiring work on Sundays -- "Remember the Sabbath and keep it Holy" caused grief. How can this be dealt with? Waiting, praying and waiting … no inspiration. How did other people deal with this seemingly dilemma? What do others think? To the library, WHAT! The library, I can't believe I am here.

Reading others struggles allowed the discovery of not being alone on an island. History allows hearing voices past giving light to the present. Finding the path well worn, discovering conversation with others today could be had with those of the past through reading.

In the process of study, I discovered who I was and there were others like me. It was in reading that I discovered the Body of Christ was more than the people at church. It was all the people of Christ, both past and present. It was in reading that I discovered a new way to live. Dangerous Wonders by Michael Yaconelli tells a story by Bill Harley about a girl called Tracy. Tracy had "coke-bottle glasses and hearing aids on each ear. She ran in a loping, carefree way, with one leg pulling after the other, one arm windmilling wildly in the air."[3] (It is a story worth the purchase price of the book.) Tracy never hit the ball in T-Ball until the last game of the season and she "smoked it right up the middle." With all the commotion, surprise, cheering and yelling Tracy rounded third headed for the game winning run. (You really need to read the story.)

Tracy discovered on her way home a "twelve-year-old geriatric mutt" with its tongue hung out and its tail wagging to be more important than a home run. Wow, with tears in my eyes, realizing I had run for home far too many times and missed what was really important in life. I discovered growth through study that day. How about you? Read anything lately that changed your life?

Prayer Life

I remember the first talk I gave on a Walk to Emmaus. Why did they select me to give the first talk? Sure, I had worked several walks, in the chapel, putting agape out, cleaning up, but never in the conference room. Going first and not knowing what to expect made me anxious. I had experience teaching classes, giving presentations, owning a business, I was a certified lay speaker in the Methodist Church, speaking in church about stewardship and setting personal priorities. None of it gave me confidence to be first out of the barrel, and it had to be a talk on priorities.

Studying the outline and researching the topic didn't calm my fears. I struggled through a draft. It read okay, but was missing something. What I thought? I shared this difficulty with friends in a reunion group, a reunion group is a small accountability group. I asked if any others had this

---
[3]Yaconelli.64

experience. They all assured me no one had this experience because none of them had given a talk. Great, why did I say yes? Then a dear older friend asked, "Have you prayed about it?" That seemed like such a given – but in fact had there been "real prayer" about the talk. Prayer for myself, time to work on the talk, praying for understanding of the outline, a place to study, patience and a whole list of other things, but had prayer been lifted up for the talk?

I set time aside to visualize the room, looking around the room, imagining people that would be listening then I asked God, "What is it that you want me to say to these folks?" My mind suddenly deluged with possibilities and the word that remained was "EVOLUTION." Great! What's that got to do with priorities I thought, "Were the people suppose to evolve?"

Pondering about this word evolution, I thought that certainly there is a priority in creation, that's when it hit me, "Mr. Potato Head". Remembering as a child putting ears, eyes, mouth and such on a potato it was the thought of taking it all off again that prompted the idea of the evolution of the rock. I realized that without proper priorities, we would slowly lose the ability and desire to do some things, thus Mr. Potato Head would lose, arms, smell, sight, sound until "just a rock." It was just what the talk needed. Everything fell into place. It all started with earnest prayer. Not prayer for me or for what I was doing, but prayer for others and God's will in this world.

How is your prayer life? Do you bring complaints, laundry lists of needs, wants, kids, spouse, church, or school to prayer? Or do you pray "Thy will be done on Earth as it is in Heaven." Can you ask, "What do you have for me today Lord, for my family, my neighborhood, my church – no your church, and your world." Then spend some time listening.

On the Road

It's that time of year again, of warm damp mornings that is cold and foggy in the low-lying areas. Driving with the windows down you can feel the change in temperature when the road drops down in a bottom. The smell noticed first, and then a slight chill touches the cheek and starts running down the back, bringing a freshness of breath that gives newness to life. The sensation is totally missed if the windows are up and the air conditioner on. I miss the vigor of this experience after giving up my motorcycle and dune buggy for primary transportation.

This smell of freshness cannot be duplicated in a can. The only way to experience it is to go out into creation and pay attention. When problems are brewing in my life, a road trip helps. Travel puts the context in flux and new dynamics surround problems and thoughts. Through the change comes the ability to focus on what is important and the less important seems to fall behind somewhere along the road. The damp freshness that attacks my breath and skin opens me up to new possibilities. Engaging in creation generates new life.

Two disciples took off for Emmaus after the crucifixion of Jesus. Were they running away from the trouble in Jerusalem? Were they going home or off to see a friend? Maybe they were carrying news of the events out to other communities. Or, maybe they needed to think. Maybe they needed to get out into creation in order to see things clearly. They traveled until they understood, and then they went back to Jerusalem to share their newfound knowledge with others.

When you discover God in creation or among others, do you go and share it or do you keep it bottled up inside as if to protect it? Are you really looking for a discovery in a can? Are you afraid the experience will dissipate if you give it to someone else? When the fresh breath of God brushes across your cheek, know that sharing will plant the event in your memory and help to keep it alive. Keep sharing. Keep living. To stop sharing with others is to die a slow death of withdrawal. Roll your windows down and go for a ride. See what creation has to offer.

Acts of Agape

The Emmaus tradition encourages people to be in an accountability group. They call it the reunion group. In my first reunion group, I met with three others – Jim, Larry and Dick. We would go through a list of questions printed on a card each week. About the third week, Larry came in and said, "After we pray for the church, I would like us to make agape." Okay, we all responded. "What would you like to make," we asked. At which Larry produced a box full of stuff.

He pulled out strings of different colors, pieces of paper with scriptures, contact paper and a box of toothpicks. Now keep in mind, Dick was a retired Ag schoolteacher and farmer. Jim retired that same year and I wasn't far behind. Larry was young and fresh. He picked up two toothpicks and in moments was wrapping them with thread.

All you have to do is hold them between your thumb and finger in the form of a cross, give the center a couple of raps, then go around each toothpick with one wrap. After five times around, tie a different color on to the string and go five more times. When you get to the outside, tie it off and leave a small piece sticking out to tie on the scripture. Then we put contact paper on the paper with the scripture and the end of the string.

It sounds easy. Larry could make ten while Jim made five. In my desire for perfection, I would pull the string tight and break half the toothpicks, requiring a restart. Therefore, I could only do three. Dick, with his arthritic hands, could do one, and it was clear he was in pain. Finally, we moved to multi-colored yarn and Popsicle sticks. Now we're talking.

The scriptures, "The eyes of the Lord are on the righteous, and his ears are open to their cry." (Psalm 34:15 NRSV) As well, "I will instruct you and teach you the way you should go; I will counsel you with my eye upon you," (Psalm 32:8 NRSV) was included. "What are we making", we asked Larry. He responded, "An Eye of God."

We did not just make agape gifts. Agape is more than doing something. The purpose behind agape gifts is not to buy or make a cute trinket or pretty picture for someone. An agape gift reflects time spent in prayer. As we wrapped string around a toothpick, we would pray for the person that would receive the gift.

Doing this is to follow in the footsteps of Christ. John tells us that Jesus prayed, "My prayer is not for them alone. I pray also for those who will believe in me through their message, that all of them may be one, Father, Just as you are in me and I am in you." (John 17:20-21b NIV) Jesus prayed for us before we were born, before we accepted God's grace, before we knew the word "Agape". Jesus prayed for us to be "At One" with God.

Agape gifts are a reflection of our time spent in prayer for those that will receive and believe. Like the Disciples and the men in the Reunion group, none looked perfect; many were crooked, off center and had visible knots. They all reflected our inability to do crafts and our broken lives. However, many people wore them with pride, not knowing who made them, but knowing that someone cared for them and prayed for them. Make something today for someone you have not yet met. Know that someone has prayed for you.

A Piece of Chicken

I go several places where I spend all day for just a few moments. It feels like such a waste of time, yet those few moments are so important. Often, I am the culprit that causes the extra time. For example, I had to see the doctor and I choose to receive my care from the VA hospital in Dallas. Therefore, I have to drive two hundred and forty miles round trip to see the doctor. That consumes five hours of my day.

There is a "side" benefit to such a long trip. The VA hospital is only six blocks from the home of my childhood. My childhood home is a few blocks from the corner of Sunnyvale and Ledbetter and on that corner is Williams Chicken. Williams Chicken opened when I was in the seventh grade, and I can still remember the first time I partook of their product. It was a most enjoyable event. Chicken that melted in my mouth and ran down the sides of my checks, covering my neck and shirt with "drippings."

I do not know how they cook or what they put in their chicken, but I feel like the owner of Williams Chicken knew

Erma Neighbors. Several years before my first experience with Williams Chicken, I was privileged to eat chicken prepared by Erma Neighbors. How tender and succulent each piece tasted. It had the lightest batter. I could tear it all off, wad it up and hold it between two fingers and pop it in my mouth. It almost melted on my tongue. Then, like Oreo cookies, the best was on the inside.

Each bite of Williams Chicken was more than a culinary experience. Each bite gave memory to another part of one of the best days of my life. I think it was Saturday, but maybe Sunday, there were Baptist, Methodist, Church of Christ and others gathered at the Neighbors' home for lunch. As far as I could tell, it was the whole world. Four by eight sheets of plywood made tables covered with bed sheets with sawhorse legs. They held plates, drinks and food. Lined up between the house and the barn it seemed like a mile from one end to the other. Boards balanced on milk cans formed seats and everyone sat at the table.

The mechanism to fill my plate provided several paths from which to choose. I could reach some items, pass my plate to someone close and they could add the item of choice. Or – I could get up, wander around the table, and hand my plate to someone who was sitting close to what I wanted and they would fill my plate. It was great, so much food and so little stomach. Everyone smiling, everyone talking, and it seemed like everyone felt good about themselves.

Conversations were many, mostly caused by passing plates. Everyone took care of everyone else. Nobody was for want and everyone had their fill. There were dogs, cats and chickens in the yard, and just a few feet over were cows with their heads pushed through the fence, eating the grass in the yard. The sounds, smells and visionary inputs put my senses on overload. All these memories came alive with each bite of Williams Chicken.

It makes me think about what Heaven might be like. Some say pearly gates and streets of gold with mansions lined up on both sides. I'm not so sure. I notice that Jesus always met people where they were, at the tax booth, up a tree, in the boat, on the shore fishing, next to the well and at the dinner table. Life is so long, and just a few moments they had to experience Jesus, but oh so important with just what is needed.

I think Heaven will have just what is needed. It may have an old white farmhouse on a dirt road. Out back in the yard will be all my friends and friends of friends sitting at a long table with the dogs, cats, chickens, cows and other animals. There will be a place at the table for me. On my plate may just be … a piece of Erma Neighbors' chicken. What will heaven be like for you? When do you feel closest to the Body of Christ?

Epilogue

It is interesting how we arrive at the uniquely created creature we are. I came to know God better and became self aware through reflecting on everyday ordinary things in life. Reflection allowed me to see that God is still speaking. God speaks through me, God speaks through you and God speaks through creation and the written word, the Bible.

My hope is reading this book has caused you to reflect on something in your life and discovered God anew. Always remember that God loves you and has prepared you for the moment that you now face. Have confidence and go forth with boldness, knowing that God goes with you. Until our path's cro†ss again, shalom.

Bibliography

Bunyan, John, and W. R. Owens. *The Pilgrim's Progress*. New ed. Oxford [England] ; New York: Oxford University Press, 2003.

Johnson, Abigail. Reflecting with God : Connecting Faith and Daily Life in Small Groups. Herndon, Va.: Alban Institute, 2004.

Nita Davis P.W., Sanderson, Terrell. "Rattlesnake on My Shirt Bosom." In *Folklore*, 7. Terrell County District NO. 19, 1936.

Rupp, Joyce, and Jane Pitz. *The Cup of Our Life : A Guide for Spiritual Growth*. Notre Dame, Ind.: Ave Maria Press, 1997.

Wink, Walter. *The Powers That Be: Theology for a New Millennium*. 1st ed. New York: Doubleday, 1998.

Yaconelli, Mike. *Dangerous Wonder : The Adventure of Childlike Faith*. [Rev. ed. Colorado Springs, Colo.: NavPress, 2003.

Index

1 Corinthians 10:32	90	Luke 9	45
1 Corinthians 3:9	33	Luke 10:27	88
1 Kings 19:4-13	57, 75	Luke 10:29	42
1 Samuel 17:4-11	94	Luke 18:24	96
1 Samuel 8:6	3	Luke 20:45ff	79
1 Thessalonians 5:16	53	Luke 23:34	76
1 Timothy 6:17-19	60	Luke 24:47	41
Acts 1:6	42	Mark 10:35-44	98
Acts 1:23–26	46	Mark 10:35f	55
Acts 2	36	Mark 16:7	41
Acts 9	7	Matthew 6:2-3	11
Acts 9:17	27	Matthew 6:24	82
Acts 12:12f	99	Mathew 14:26	66
Acts 14:17	74	Matthew 10:21	97
Acts 16:14	64	Matthew 10:30	51
Daniel 3:16-18	48	Matthew 11:28	72
Ecclesiastes 3:1	41	Matthew 12:38-44	79
Ecclesiastes 12:13	88	Matthew 13:44	17
Exodus 3	2	Matthew 14:13	75
Exodus 31:1	22	Matthew 16:23	31
Exodus 34	25	Matthew 16:24	93
Galations 5:6	23	Matthew 18:20	59
Galations 6:1	28	Matthew 20:20-28	98
Isaiah 1:16b-17	42	Matthew 21:15	59
Isaiah 40:1	63	Matthew 21:42	87
Isaiah 41:1	73	Matthew 26:36ff	70
Isaiah 56:7	59	Matthew 28:19	41
Jeremiah 29:11	58	Micah 6:8	20
John 3:16	49	Philemon 2:3	19
John 17:20	76	Philippians 4:13	58, 93
John 17:20-21b	106	Philippians 4:6	82
John 21:15	59	Psalm 32:8	105
John 21:17	43	Psalm 34:15	105
John 21:22	41	Psalm 63:1	17
Judges	38	Psalm 67:1-2	18
Luke 6:12	70	Psalm 84:2	51

Psalm 91:2-4	31
Psalm 139:4	29
Revelation 22:17	15, 33, 41, 63
Romans 8:26	2
Romans 14:19	89

www.ingramcontent.com/pod-product-compliance
Lightning Source LLC
LaVergne TN
LVHW052255070426
835507LV00035B/2917

9781603500081